FIRST THE RAPTURE

J.F. Strombeck

HARVEST HOUSE PUBLISHERS
Eugene, Oregon 97402

FIRST THE RAPTURE

Copyright ©1982 Harvest House Publishers
Eugene, Oregon 97402
Originally published in 1950 by the Strombeck Foundation.
Library of Congress Catalog Card Number 81-85528
ISBN 0-89081-309-4

Printed in the United States of America.

FOREWORD

When I was a very young believer, someone introduced me to the books written by J.F. Strombeck, and I bless the day it happened. SHALL NEVER PERISH settled for me the matter of my security in Christ, and GRACE AND TRUTH helped me understand the true relationship between law and grace. DISCIPLINED BY GRACE balanced these doctrines for me and delivered me from the extremes some people go to when they first discover grace and assurance. I owe a debt of gratitude to Mr. Strombeck, and I gladly acknowledge it.

John Frederick Strombeck was born in Moline, Illinois, on December 16, 1881, into a pioneer Swedish family. Converted to Christ early in life, J.F. always sought God's leading in his decisions, both personal and business.

He started his own freight auditing business, which he managed for about ten years. When he was 25, he returned to school, first at Northwestern Academy, and then Northwestern University, from which he graduated Phi Beta Kappa in 1911. After his graduation, the Strombeck-Becker Manufacturing Company was born, specializing in various wood products. That same year he married.

J.F.'s first love was ministry in the church and with various Christian organizations that he supported. He served as a director or advisor to the Belgian Gospel Mission, Dallas Theological Seminary, Moody Bible Institute, Young Life, Inter-Varsity, and many others. While a member of the Evangelical Free Church, he was often invited to minister in the Word in various conferences, and he wrote many articles for Christian publications. The burden of foreign missions lay heavy on his heart, and he was a generous supporter of missionaries and schools that trained missionaries.

You will discover as you read each of his books that J.F. Strombeck, though a layman, had a thorough grasp of Bible doctrine and was able to apply it practically. He did not write books in order to *impress,* but to *express* what God taught him, so that you might enjoy the full blessings of salvation in Christ. I suggest that you keep your Bible close at hand as you read Strombeck's books, because he uses the Word from beginning to end!

Though J.F. Strombeck died on May 9, 1959, the investments he made in many evangelical ministries continue to produce spiritual dividends, and his Christ-centered books continue to challenge and instruct serious students of the Word. I rejoice that Harvest House is making these helpful volumes available to a new generation of believers.

WARREN W. WIERSBE

FIRST THE RAPTURE

Preface

THE present is an age of great anxiety because of the catastrophic events that have been predicted. The late H. G. Wells is quoted as having said, "This world is at the end of its tether. The end of everything we call life is close at hand." A great general has said, "We have had our last chance. Armageddon is at hand," and the governor of a great state has said, "At least 90% of all Americans now living will be killed by atom bombs within five years."

The fulfillment of these predictions can be nothing less than the great tribulation foretold by Jesus in the Olivet discourse. "The end of everything we call life" would surely come but for the words of Jesus, "And except those days should be shortened, there should no flesh be saved: but for the elect's sake those days shall be shortened" (Matt. 24:22).

All who believe in the imminent coming of the Lord to catch up His Church need have no fear for "those days" because that event shall transpire before these things come upon the inhabitants of the earth.

The purpose of this book is to bring assurance and peace to the hearts of true believers at a time when so many are proclaiming that the Church will go through the tribulation. It has been written with the encouragement of several outstanding evangelical leaders and with the co-operation of a number of Bible scholars well versed in theology and in the original Greek and Hebrew texts. It is hoped that the reading hereof may result in a greater longing and "Looking for that blessed hope, and the glorious appearing of the great God and our Saviour Jesus Christ" (Titus 2:13).

Moline, Illinois   J. F. S.

Contents

CHAPTER 1

Introduction

SHORTLY before Jesus left this world to go to His Father He promised His disciples that He would return. He said, "I will come again, and receive you unto myself; that where I am, there ye may be also" (John 14:3). This promise was later confirmed to the Church through the Apostle Paul.

This promise of the Lord's return to receive the Church unto Himself has been set before the Church as a blessed hope. It is something for which the Church should eagerly wait, expecting Him to come at any moment.

This promise is one of the most important notes in the apostolic letters to the Church. It has been set forth as an incentive to purity of life, to patience, to hope, to a labor of love, to endurance, and to holiness, as well as to other virtues of the Christian life. In fact, the *looking* for His glorious appearing is said to be as essential a part of the believer's life as to deny ungodliness and worldly lust and to live soberly, righteously, and godly in the present world (Titus 2:12–13). Nothing should be allowed to distract attention from this glorious prospect.

Conditions in the world today indicate that the present age is rapidly drawing to a close. Men of the world predict that the lights of civilization are going out, that most of those living today shall be dead within a very few years. The chaotic condition of the world is beyond human solution.

On the other hand, the beginning of the fulfillment of the promises of the restoration of Palestine to Israel is already seen. Because of these, it is certain that the time on earth for the Church must be short. The fulfillment of the promise to come again must be very near at hand. This should be a great stimulus for the Church to an even more intensive waiting and looking for His coming.

But a strange voice is being heard, one that is disturbing and distracting to many who are or have been looking with joy toward the soon coming of the Lord. Men are teaching that the Church cannot look for the imminent coming of Christ. He cannot come immediately. The Church must first pass through that time of tribulation, so terrible that the like has never been before nor ever shall be thereafter. It is said that not until after that awful time has passed over the Church will the promise of Jesus to His disciples be fulfilled. This teaching is called the post-tribulation view of the rapture.

Some are not willing to say that the Church shall pass through all of this period. Because they see in it the wrath of God, especially in the last half, an effort is made to locate the rapture in the middle of that period. This is the mid-tribulation view of the rapture. But this also destroys the daily looking for the Lord's return. If this view is right the rapture cannot come before three and a half years after a covenant has been made by some political ruler allowing the Jews to re-establish their worship in Jerusalem.

The purpose of this small volume is to examine carefully what God's Word has to say in support of the imminent coming of the Lord to catch the Church up to be with Him before the tribulation begins. This is the pre-tribulation view.

An appalling ignorance of the reason the rapture shall come before the tribulation is found among true believers. Altogether too much is being taken for granted because that view is the prevailing one of the group with which one fellowships, or because certain Bible teachers hold that view. Little, yes, very little, is known of what the Bible teaches. This is one reason, probably the greatest, for the disturbed feeling and why many are willing to exchange the blessed hope of seeing Christ before the tribulation for the post-tribulation view.

In the approach to the study of this subject one rule must be laid down as basic. What do the Scriptures say? No recent or contemporary events or circumstances can be admitted as proof. In the interpretation of Scripture passages having two or more possible meanings, only those meanings confirmed by other passages can be accepted as valid. Interpretations of such passages by learned men and great scholars cannot be taken as final. Men's interpretations depend largely upon the viewpoint from which a subject is approached.

One rule of Bible interpretation is of exceptional

importance in this study. There must be a clear recognition of whom or to whom any passage is written. Some things are addressed to Israel or about them. Others have the Church in view. Still others are for the Gentiles. Those applying to Israel must not be ascribed to the Church. This demands an understanding of God's purposes for Israel, for the Church, and for the Gentiles. Apart from this understanding it is impossible to interpret properly many passages that are met within the present study.

Many words or expressions must be defined or clarified. As the discussion revolves around the Church, it is important to know that, as here used, it includes only those who have been born again by the Spirit of God. It does not include mere professors of Christianity or church members. The name *saint* is applied to God's people of the Old Testament, to the Church, to those saved during the tribulation, and to the faithful of Israel who shall go through the tribulation. Likewise the name *elect* is applied to God's chosen people, Israel, just as it is to the members of the Church. Failure to recognize this has led to wrong conclusions.

Certain periods of time together with the meaning of each and what God has planned for each must be recognized, as, for example, the day of the Lord, the day of Jacob's trouble, the seventieth week of Israel, the Church age or the age of grace, the tribulation, and the Messianic kingdom. God's purpose in any one of these must not be confused with His purposes in some other period.

The Old Testament prophets, and Jesus Himself in the Synoptic Gospels, tell of a future coming of the Lord to deal with the sinful conditions of men and to set up a kingdom of righteousness on earth. Jesus, in the Gospel according to John, promised to come again to receive believers unto Himself in heaven. This coming is also foretold and repeatedly referred to in the epistles to the Church. These two must never be confused with each other.

The following chapters are intended to bring a helpful understanding of all of these terms and to present arguments, based on the Bible, to prove the pre-tribulation view of the rapture.

The first part of the book is devoted to the direct teaching on the subject. In the second part answers are given to many of the arguments by the mid- and post-tribulation advocates. These are given to help any who may be confused by their teachings. Part two is not intended to be an exhaustive study of all post-tribulation arguments. It is rather illustrative of the methods used to arrive at that view.

CHAPTER 2

The Lord's Second Advent to the Earth

IN THE Old Testament are many prophecies which tell of the coming of the Lord in person to this earth. These are addressed to God's people, Israel, and the place to be visited by Him is their land, Palestine.

Many of these prophecies were fulfilled when the Son of God came to earth and as a man lived within the boundaries of Palestine for thirty-three years, and then was crucified by the Romans at the urgent demand of the Jewish people. Because of many other prophecies which were not then fulfilled a second advent is still in the future.

Among the last words of Moses to Israel is found this great promise: "The LORD thy God . . . will return and gather thee from all the nations, whither the LORD thy God hath scattered thee. If any of thine be driven out unto the outmost parts of heaven, from thence will the LORD thy God gather thee, and from thence will he fetch thee: and the LORD thy God will bring thee into the land which thy fathers possessed, and thou shalt possess it; and he will do thee good, and multiply thee above thy fathers" (Deut. 30:3–5).

This is a promise that the Lord God will return and regather Israel and bring them to Palestine. All of this is still in the future.

Another prophecy is found in the second Psalm: "Yet have I set my king upon my holy hill of Zion. . . . Thou [the King] shalt break them [the heathen] with a rod of iron; thou shalt dash them in pieces like a potter's vessel" (vs. 6, 9). Here the earthly picture develops. The Lord is seen as King seated on Mount Zion and ruling the Gentile nations with a rod of iron.

Additional detail of the earthly rule of the Lord is given in Psalm 96:13: "For he cometh to judge the earth: he shall judge the world with righteousness, and the people with his truth." Isaiah adds: "Of the increase of his government and peace there shall be no end, upon the throne of David, and upon his kingdom, to order it, and to establish it with judgment and with justice from henceforth even forever" (Isa. 9:7). The Lord's earthly rule, then, shall be a continuation of the house of King David.

Jeremiah also prophesied the coming of the Lord to rule over an earthly kingdom. "Behold, the days come, saith the LORD, that I will raise unto David a righteous Branch, and a King shall reign and prosper, and shall execute judgment and justice in the earth. In his days Judah shall be saved, and Israel shall dwell safely" (Jer. 23:5–6).

The Lord told Ezekiel to say to his people: "Behold, I will take the children of Israel from among the heathen, whither they be gone, and will gather them on every side, and bring them into their own land: and I will make them one nation in the land upon the mountains of Israel; and one king shall be

king to them all: and they shall be no more two nations, neither shall they be divided into two kingdoms any more at all" (Ezek. 37:21–22).

In view of the present recognition of Israel as a
nation in Palestine, does anyone now dare to say that
these prophecies shall not be literally fulfilled? They
cannot be construed as finding a fulfillment in the
Church. This promised kingdom shall be earthly beyond any doubt.

Daniel in his night vision saw "one like the Son of
man come with the clouds of heaven. . . . And
there was given him dominion, and glory, and a
kingdom, that all people, nations, and languages,
should serve him" (Dan. 7:13–14). The name "Son
of man" is here, for the first time, applied to Him
who is to rule over the earthly kingdom of Israel and
the nations of the world.

A future Davidic kingdom for Israel is foretold by
Hosea. "For the children of Israel shall abide many
days without a king, and without a prince. . . .
Afterward shall the children of Israel return, and
seek the LORD their God, and David their king . . .
in the latter days" (Hos. 3:4–5). Micah added his
voice to the others and said, "The LORD shall reign
over them in mount Zion from henceforth, even for
ever" (Micah 4:7).

The prophet Zechariah confirms that which has
been spoken by the other prophets and adds certain
details. "Sing and rejoice, O daughter of Zion: for,
lo, I come, and I will dwell in the midst of thee,
saith the LORD. . . . And the LORD shall inherit

Judah his portion in the holy land, and shall choose Jerusalem again" (Zech. 2:10, 12). Jerusalem is to be chosen *again*. This, then, must be the historic Jerusalem.

"Behold, the day of the LORD cometh, and thy spoil shall be divided in the midst of thee. For I will gather all nations against Jerusalem to battle; and the city shall be taken, and the houses rifled, and the women ravished; and half of the city shall go forth into captivity, and the residue of the people shall not be cut off from the city. Then shall the LORD go forth, and fight against those nations. . . . And his feet shall stand in that day upon the mount of Olives, which is before Jerusalem on the east, and the mount of Olives shall cleave in the midst thereof toward the east and toward the west. . . . The LORD my God shall come, and all the saints with thee" (Zech. 14:1-5).

Malachi brings the last Old Testament prophecy of an advent of the Lord which must still be in the future. "For, behold, the day cometh that shall burn as an oven; and all the proud, yea, and all that do wickedly, shall be stubble: and the day that cometh shall burn them up, saith the LORD of hosts, that it shall leave them neither root nor branch. But unto you that fear my name shall the Sun of righteousness arise with healing in his wings; and ye [Israel] shall go forth, and grow up as calves of the stall" (Mal. 4:1-2). The Sun of righteousness can be none other than He who is "the true Light, which lighteth every man that cometh into the world" (John 1:9), and

who said, "I am the light of the world" (John 8:12).
When the wicked are being destroyed then shall the
Sun of righteousness bring healing unto Israel.

These passages, and others not quoted here, show
that the unanimous testimony of the Old Testament
prophets, from Moses to Malachi, covering a period
of about a thousand years, foretold an advent of the
Lord which is still in the future. Their combined
prophecies are an assurance that the Lord shall return bodily to this earth. His feet shall stand on the
Mount of Olives. He shall make war upon the nations of the world and destroy them. He shall re-
establish and sit upon the throne of David in Jerusalem. In these prophecies is an assurance that Israel
shall be brought back into Palestine in which their
fathers lived. They shall be healed of their sins and
live in peace, serving the Lord. All this shall take
place upon the earth. It all belongs to Israel, God's
chosen people of Old Testament times.

It is approximately 2,500 years since Judah had a
king. While Israel has now been restored as a nation
among the nations of the earth, they still have no
king. They cannot have one until He who is both
Son and Lord of David returns. All genealogies have
been lost and none other can claim the right to sit on
David's throne.

Turning now to the pages of the Synoptic Gospels, one finds many statements which unmistakably
teach that Jesus Christ shall return from heaven. In
the Gospel according to Matthew are statements by

Jesus Himself which are in perfect agreement with those already quoted.

When Peter asked Jesus what they should have because they had forsaken all and followed Him, He said: "Ye which have followed me, in the regeneration when the Son of man shall sit in the throne of his glory, ye also shall sit upon twelve thrones, judging the twelve tribes of Israel" (Matt. 19:28). Here the Lord associates the throne of His glory with Israel, not the Church.

In His lament over Jerusalem Jesus said: "Ye shall not see me henceforth, till ye shall say, Blessed is he that cometh in the name of the Lord" (Matt. 23:39).

As Jesus sat on the Mount of Olives His disciples asked, "What shall be the sign of thy coming?" He replied: "Then shall be great tribulation, such as was not since the beginning of the world to this time, no, nor ever shall be. . . . Immediately after the tribulation of those days shall the sun be darkened, and the moon shall not give her light, and the stars shall fall from heaven, and the powers of the heavens shall be shaken: and then shall appear the sign of the Son of man in heaven: and then shall all the tribes of the earth mourn, and they shall see the Son of man coming in the clouds of heaven with power and great glory. And he shall send his angels with a great sound of a trumpet, and they shall gather his elect from the four winds, from one end of heaven to the other" (Matt. 24:21, 29–31).

This statement, by the Lord, confirms the promise made to Israel through Moses: "The LORD thy God . . . will return and gather thee from all the nations, whither the LORD thy God hath scattered thee. If any of thine be driven out unto the outmost parts of heaven, from thence will the LORD thy God gather thee, and from thence will he fetch thee." The elect according to Isaiah 65:9, 22 are the seed of Jacob (Israel) re-established in Palestine.

Numerous passages mention that Israel will be gathered back to Palestine from the nations of the earth. Two are here quoted: "And he . . . shall assemble the outcasts of Israel, and gather together the dispersed of Judah from the four corners of the earth" (Isa. 11:12). "Fear not: for I am with thee: I will bring thy seed from the east, and gather thee from the west; I will say to the north, Give up; and to the south, Keep not back: bring my sons from far, and my daughters from the ends of the earth" (Isa. 43:5–6).

Again in Matthew is found another scene which has its setting on the earth. "When the Son of man shall come in his glory, and all the holy angels with him, then shall he sit upon the throne of his glory: and before him shall be gathered all nations" (Matt. 25:31–32a). This must be on the earth because there are no nations in heaven.

The preceding passages clearly teach that the Lord shall with power and great glory return to the earth. He shall regather and restore Israel and sitting on David's throne, rule over them, as well as over the nations on the entire earth. In none of these passages is found the least reference to the Church. This is so because the Church belongs to another sphere, and the promises to her of the Lord's return are quite different as will be seen in the next chapter.

This advent of the Lord to the earth is definitely timed as taking place immediately after the days of tribulation that shall come upon the earth.

CHAPTER 3

Christ's Coming for the Church

I N THE Upper Room when Jesus met with His disciples the last time before the cross He spoke in simple but impressive words concerning His coming again. "Let not your heart be troubled: ye believe in God, believe also in me. In my Father's house are many mansions: if it were not so, I would have told you. I go to prepare a place for you. And if I go and prepare a place for you, I will come again, and receive you unto myself; that where I am, there ye may be also" (John 14:1–3).

How different these words are from those spoken to the disciples in the Olivet Discourse as recorded by Matthew! "When the Son of man shall come in his glory, and all the holy angels with him, then shall he sit upon the throne of his glory: and before him shall be gathered all nations: and he shall separate them one from another, as a shepherd divideth his sheep from the goats" (Matt. 25:31–32).

And how different from the Old Testament prophecies! "God will bring thee [Israel] into the land." "I have set my king upon the holy hill of Zion." "Our God shall come . . . a fire shall devour before him and it shall be very tempestuous before him." "For he cometh to judge the earth." "A king shall reign and prosper and execute judgment and justice upon the earth." "I will take the children of Israel and bring them . . . into their own land." "The LORD shall reign over them [Israel] in mount Zion."

The difference between Jesus' comforting words to the disciples and the Old Testament prophecies and His own statements concerning His return is as the difference between heaven and earth. In no statement in the Old Testament or the Synoptic Gospels is a heavenly position promised in connection with the Lord's return. All judgments and all blessings apply to an earthly position.

On the contrary there is not the slightest room for injecting an earthly position into the promise made to the eleven disciples. This promise is concerned with "my Father's house" and the many mansions in heaven to which He went to make preparation for their coming to Him.

Jesus said, "I" will come again to receive you. He will not send His holy angels to bring the Church to heaven. His promise is to come in person to escort His own to the mansions of the Father's house.

"That where I am, there ye may be also," speaks of a fellowship with Him. This fellowship is not like the relationship of servants to a master, nor of subjects to a king as Israel shall be when He sits on the throne of David in Jerusalem. It is on the most intimate relationship of friendship. A few brief moments earlier in the evening He had said to the same disciples: "Henceforth I call you not servants; for the servant knoweth not what his lord doeth: but

I have called you friends; for all things that I have heard of my Father I have made known unto you" (John 15:15). Yes, it means to be with Him as friends, hearing from Him even more fully the things the Father has made known to Him.

In His prayer to His Father, as recorded by John, He declared: "I will that they also, whom thou hast given me, be with me where I am; that they may behold my glory, which thou hast given me" (17:24).

That this applies to the Church, to all believers, is made clear by verse 20. "Neither pray I for these alone, but for them also which shall believe on me through their word." The one condition for becoming a member of the true Church and being with Him in glory is to believe on Him.

In the words, "I will come again, and receive you unto myself," is introduced an entirely new thought in connection with the coming of the Lord. Neither in the Old Testament nor in the Synoptic Gospels is there the least suggestion that He will come to bring His own, those given Him by His Father, into heaven. It follows, then, that the coming of the Lord means something vastly more for the Church than it does for Israel who are to remain on earth to receive His blessings.

While the disciples looked steadfastly toward heaven as Christ was taken up in a cloud, two men, in white apparel, stood by them and said: "Ye men of Galilee, why stand ye gazing up into heaven? this same Jesus, which is taken up from you into heaven, shall so come in like manner as ye have seen him go up into heaven" (Acts 1:11).

Here, by the two men in white apparel, is reiterated the promise by Jesus, "if I go . . . I will come again." In addition, they declare in unmistakable words how He shall come. "This same Jesus . . . shall so come in like manner as ye have seen him go up into heaven." It was a visible going up. It shall be a visible return. He went up in a cloud. He shall return in the cloud. He was seen going up alone. He shall come alone for the Church.

These words cannot, without doing violence to them, be construed as Christ coming for His own in physical death. When the spirit of the one who falls asleep in Christ is conveyed into the presence of the Lord there is no visible coming of Christ as He was seen ascending into heaven. This coming is something still in the future and is for all believers. It is for the eleven disciples and all who are to believe because of their word.

In 1 Thessalonians 4:15–17 Paul declared: "The Lord himself shall descend from heaven with a shout, with the voice of the archangel, and with the trump of God: and the dead in Christ shall rise first: then we which are alive and remain shall be caught up together with them in the clouds, to meet the Lord in the air: and so shall we ever be with the Lord."

The statement, "The Lord himself shall descend from heaven," re-emphasizes Jesus' own words to His disciples, "I will come again." The expression, "the Lord himself," is said by scholars to be much stronger in the original text. It means "The Lord, he himself and no other." This is in harmony with Jesus' promise to His disciples, "I will . . . receive you unto myself." The importance of this is seen when the great purpose of His coming is realized.

When the Lord descends with a shout "the dead in Christ shall rise first," just as it was in the day of His earthly life when "he cried with a loud voice, Lazarus come forth," and Lazarus arose. It is important to notice that it is the "dead in Christ." It is all those who have become new creatures by being in Him. Nothing is here said about the wicked dead.

As the dead in Christ are raised, "Then we [all who belong to the Church] which are alive and remain shall be caught up together with them in the clouds, to meet the Lord in the air." This meeting is to be "in the air." The Lord does not come to the earth on this occasion. His feet do not stand on the Mount of Olives as they shall do when He comes to save Israel and set up His kingdom on earth.

"So shall we ever be with the Lord." This is as Jesus promised the disciples. It shall be an unending state.

Why must He Himself and no other come? Because it is the Church, His body, that shall be gathered unto Him. It is the Church that He has loved and cleansed by the washing of water by the word, "That he might present it to himself a glorious church, not having spot, or wrinkle, or any such thing; but that it should be holy and without blemish" (Eph. 5:25–27). It is the chaste virgin, espoused unto Christ, that is to be presented to Him.

No angels are sent to gather the Church unto Him from the four winds as is true of the elect of Israel (Matt. 24:31). He is not even to be accompanied by all the holy angels as He will be when He comes to sit upon the throne of His glory (Matt. 25:31). He Himself and none other shall come to bring His bride into the many dwelling places of the Father's house.

"And so shall we ever be with the Lord." This shall be an unending glorious fellowship with Him.

These passages speak of a return of the Lord Jesus Christ to bring His Church unto Himself in heaven and there to dwell with Him forever. The same intimacy that is seen in His promise to the disciples is also seen here.

Two things occur simultaneously at this coming of the Lord: a resurrection of the dead in Christ, and the catching up of the living believers with them.

How different this description of His coming is from that described in Chapter 2. There it is set forth that He comes to gather Israel into the land, Palestine. Here, He comes to bring to heaven those who believe on Him through the word of the disciples. There, He comes with all the holy angels. Here, He comes alone. There, the angels do the gathering of Israel. Here, He Himself and no other, does the gathering together unto Himself the

Church. There, He comes to earth, His feet resting on the Mount of Olives. Here, the Church meets Him in the air. When He comes in the clouds of heaven with power and great glory, all the tribes of the earth shall mourn (Matt. 24:30). "All kindreds of the earth shall wail because of him" (Rev. 1:7). Yes, Israel also shall look upon Him "whom they have pierced, and they shall mourn for him, as one mourneth for his only son" (Zech. 12:10). When His glory shall be revealed the Church shall "be glad . . . with exceeding joy" (1 Pet. 4:13).

These revelations of His coming are so different that they fully justify the conclusion that they describe two separate and distinct events.

It has already been seen that His coming to Israel is to be immediately after the great tribulation. The time of His coming for the Church will be considered later, but first there must be a clear understanding of the relative position of Israel and the Church and God's purpose with each. A lack of clear understanding of God's program for the Jews, the Gentiles, and the Church of Christ is the cause of much misunderstanding about the time of this important event.

CHAPTER 4

The Day of the Lord

IT is impossible to understand rightly two of the
most important Scripture passages that throw
light on the time of the rapture, without an adequate
understanding of the meaning and extent of that
period of time which is known as "the day of the
Lord." It is therefore necessary to trace throughout
the Bible that which is said about that day. The following are portions of some important prophecies
descriptive thereof.

"For the day of the LORD of hosts shall be upon
every one that is proud and lofty, and upon every
one that is lifted up; and he shall be brought low.
And they shall go into the holes of the rocks, and into
the caves of the earth, for fear of the LORD, and for
the glory of his majesty, when he ariseth to shake
terribly the earth" (Isa. 2:12, 19).

"Behold, the day of the LORD cometh, cruel both
with wrath and fierce anger, to lay the land desolate:
and he shall destroy the sinners thereof out of it.
For the stars of heaven and the constellations thereof
shall not give their light: the sun shall be darkened
in his going forth, and the moon shall not cause her
light to shine. And I will punish the world for their
evil, and the wicked for their iniquity; and I will
cause the arrogancy of the proud to cease, and will

lay low the haughtiness of the terrible. I will shake the heavens, and the earth shall remove out of her place, in the wrath of the LORD of hosts, and in the day of his fierce anger" (Isa. 13:9–11, 13).

"Come, my people, enter thou into thy chambers, and shut thy doors about thee: hide thyself as it were for a little moment, until the indignation be overpast. For, behold, the LORD cometh out of his place to punish the inhabitants of the earth for their iniquity" (Isa. 26:20–21).

"Come near, ye nations, to hear; and hearken ye people: . . . For the indignation of the LORD is upon all nations, and his fury upon all their armies: he hath utterly destroyed them, he hath delivered them to the slaughter. For it is the day of the LORD's vengeance" (Isa. 34:1–2, 8).

"Son of man, prophesy and say, . . . Howl ye, Woe worth the day! For the day is near, even the day of the LORD is near, a cloudy day; it shall be the time of the heathen" (Ezek. 30:2–3).

"Alas for the day! for the day of the LORD is at hand, and as a destruction from the Almighty shall it come" (Joel 1:15).

"Blow ye the trumpet in Zion, and sound an alarm in my holy mountain: let all the inhabitants of the land tremble: for the day of the LORD cometh, for it is nigh at hand; a day of darkness and of gloominess, a day of clouds and thick darkness, . . . there hath not been ever the like, neither shall be any more after it, even to the years of many generations. A fire devoureth before them; and behind them a flame burneth: the land is as the garden of Eden before them, and behind them a desolate wilderness; yea, and nothing shall escape them" (Joel 2:1–3).

"And I will shew wonders in the heavens and in the earth, blood, and fire, and pillars of smoke. The sun shall be turned into darkness, and the moon into blood, before the great and terrible day of the LORD come. And it shall come to pass, that whosoever shall call on the name of the LORD shall be delivered: for in mount Zion and in Jerusalem shall be deliverance, as the LORD hath said, and in the remnant whom the Lord shall call" (Joel 2:30–32).

"Let the heathen be wakened, and come up to the valley of Jehoshaphat: for there will I sit to judge all the heathen round about. Put in the sickle, for the harvest is ripe: come, get you down; for the press is full, the fats overflow; for their wickedness is great. Multitudes, multitudes in the valley of decision: for the day of the LORD is near in the valley of decision. The sun and the moon shall be darkened, and the stars shall withdraw their shining. The LORD also shall roar out of Zion, and utter his voice from Jerusalem; and the heavens and the earth shall shake: but the LORD will be the hope of his people, and the strength of the children of Israel. And it shall come to pass in that day, that the mountains shall drop down new wine, and the hills shall flow with milk, and all the rivers of Judah shall flow with water, and a fountain shall come forth of the house of the LORD, and shall water the valley of Shittim" (Joel 3:12–16, 18).

"Woe unto you that desire the day of the Lord! to what end is it for you? the day of the Lord is darkness, and not light. Shall not the day of the Lord be darkness, and not light? even very dark, and no brightness in it?" (Amos 5:18, 20).

"For the day of the Lord is near upon all the heathen. . . . They shall be as though they had not been. But upon mount Zion shall be deliverance, and there shall be holiness; and the house of Jacob shall possess their possessions" (Obad. vs. 15–17).

"The great day of the Lord is near, it is near, and hasteth greatly, even the voice of the day of the Lord: the mighty man shall cry there bitterly. That day is a day of wrath, a day of trouble and distress, a day of wasteness and desolation, a day of darkness and gloominess, a day of clouds and thick darkness. I will bring distress upon men, that they shall walk like blind men, because they have sinned against the Lord: and their blood shall be poured out as dust, and their flesh as the dung" (Zeph. 1:14–15, 17).

"Behold, I will make Jerusalem a cup of trembling unto all the people round about, when they shall be in the siege both against Judah and against Jerusalem. And it shall come to pass in that day, that I will seek to destroy all the nations that come against Jerusalem. And I will pour upon the house of David, and upon the inhabitants of Jerusalem, the spirit of grace and of supplications: and they shall look upon me whom they have pierced, and they shall mourn for him, as one mourneth for his only son, and shall

be in bitterness for him, as one that is in bitterness
for his firstborn" (Zech. 12:2, 9, 10).

"Behold, the day of the LORD cometh. . . . For I
will gather all nations against Jerusalem to battle.
. . . Then shall the LORD go forth, and fight against
those nations, as when he fought in the day of battle.
And his feet shall stand in that day upon the mount
of Olives, which is before Jerusalem on the east.
. . . And the LORD my God shall come and all the
saints with thee. And it shall be in that day, that living waters shall go out from Jerusalem; . . . And
the LORD shall be king over all the earth: in that day
shall there be one LORD, and his name one. In that
day shall there be upon the bells of the horses, HOLI-
NESS UNTO THE LORD" (Zech. 14:1–5, 8–9, 20).

"For, behold, the day cometh, that shall burn as
an oven; and all the proud, yea, and all that do
wickedly, shall be stubble: and the day that cometh
shall burn them up, saith the LORD of hosts, that it
shall leave them neither root nor branch. But unto
you that fear my name shall the Sun of righteousness
arise with healing in his wings; and ye shall go forth,
and grow up as calves of the stall" (Mal. 4:1–3).

Paul dramatically described the beginning of the
day of the Lord in these words: "The day of the Lord
so cometh as a thief in the night. For when they shall
say, Peace and safety; then sudden destruction
cometh upon them, as travail upon a woman with
child; and they shall not escape" (1 Thess. 5:2–3). In
this is seen a period of apparent peace. But it is a
time of false security because of impending sudden

destruction. It is important to remember this description by Paul of the beginning of the day of the Lord.

More could be quoted in explanation of the day of the Lord, as the Messianic rule with its blessings for Israel and the Gentile nations. Because these have no bearing on the time of the rapture, they are here omitted.

Peter also wrote of the day of the Lord. He preceded his comments by the words: "But, beloved, be not ignorant of this one thing, that one day is with the Lord as a thousand years, and a thousand years as one day." Then he wrote: "But the day of the Lord will come as a thief in the night; in the which the heavens shall pass away with a great noise, and the elements shall melt with fervent heat, the earth also and the works that are therein shall be burned up" (2 Pet. 3:8, 10). This passing away of the heavens and earth must come at the end of the Messianic reign. All this is evidence that the day of the Lord shall continue for a thousand years.

The above quotations describe certain aspects of the day of the Lord which must be recognized in determining the time of the rapture.

1. It shall come with unexpected suddenness upon the dwellers on the earth at a time "when they shall say, Peace and safety"—a time of false security.

2. That day shall come as a destruction from the Lord; and as a devouring fire. It shall be a day of trouble and distress. It is the day of wrath and fierce anger and of the Lord's vengeance.

3. It shall be a day of clouds, a day of gloom and darkness, even thick darkness. The stars of heaven and the constellations thereof shall not give their light. The sun shall be darkened and the moon turned to blood. The heavens and the earth shall be shaken and the earth removed out of her place.

4. The indignation of the Lord shall be upon all people. The Lord shall punish the world for their evil and the wicked for their iniquity. He shall bring distress upon men because they have sinned against Him.

5. The day of the Lord shall be the day of Jacob's trouble. Sinners of Israel shall be destroyed out of the land. It shall be a day of purging before the Son of man comes in the clouds of heaven.

6. But deliverance shall come in Mount Zion and Jerusalem in the remnant of Israel. The Lord shall be the hope of His people and the strength of Israel. Their land shall be blessed and the house of Jacob shall possess their possessions.

7. Israel shall see Him whom they have pierced and mourn as one mourneth for the only son. Unto those who fear His name shall the Sun of righteousness appear with healing under His wings. The feet of the Lord shall stand upon the Mount of Olives and living waters shall go out from Jerusalem. Jesus said that after the tribulation the Son of man shall come in the clouds of heaven with power and great glory. Then the Messianic kingdom shall be established and the Lord shall be King over all the earth.

CHAPTER 5

The Tribulation

As a help in understanding whether the resurrection and rapture of the Church saints shall take place before or after the tribulation, it is well to know something of the exact nature of that time. Can the teachings concerning the Church, its present position, and its future destiny, be harmonized with the view that she shall pass through the tribulation? Will God's purposes for the Church, both on earth and in heaven, be furthered thereby? Would this in any way purify or add anything to the Church? These and other questions are more easily answered if one has an understanding of that time.

A time of fierce anger and wrath of God upon man was foreseen as a part of the day of the Lord by several of the Old Testament prophets. One of them, Daniel, foresaw a time of unprecedented trouble such as has never been before. "And at that time shall Michael stand up, the great prince which standeth for the children of thy people: and there shall be a time of trouble, such as never was since there was a nation even to that same time: and at that time thy people shall be delivered, every one that shall be found written in the book" (Dan. 12:1). Speaking of the same time about which Daniel wrote Jesus said in His Olivet discourse: "For then shall be great tribulation, such as was not since the beginning of the world to this time, no, nor ever shall be. And except those days should be shortened, there should no flesh be saved: but for the elect's sake those days shall be shortened" (Matt. 24:21–22). No time in history can be compared with the coming tribulation.

In Revelation is found the full description of the tribulation. In John's vision it commenced when the Lamb opened the first of the seals of the seven-sealed book. Then John heard thunder and saw a rider on a white horse and with a bow go forth "conquering, and to conquer." Here is seen a period of armed peace, a time of false security. It must be so because the second rider was seen to take peace from the earth, and men killed one another. Here is war, and that of great magnitude because of the great sword that was given this rider.

The third rider, on the black horse, brought famine, and the fourth rider, on a pale horse, was given power "over the fourth part of the earth, to kill with sword, and with hunger, and with death, and with the beasts of the earth." World Wars I and II pale into insignificance compared with the carnage of that time which is to come.

When the sixth seal was opened "there was a great earthquake; and the sun became black as sackcloth of hair, and the moon became as blood; and the stars of heaven fell unto the earth, even as a fig tree casteth her untimely figs, when she is shaken of a mighty wind. And the heaven departed as a scroll when it is rolled together; and every mountain and island were moved out of their places. And the kings of the earth, and the great men, and the rich men, and the chief captains, and the mighty men, and every bond-man, and every free man, hid themselves in the dens and in the rocks of the mountains; and said to the mountains and rocks, Fall on us, and hide us from the face of him that sitteth on the throne, and from the wrath of the Lamb: for the great day of his wrath is come; and who shall be able to stand?" (6:12–17).

In continuing the enumeration of the things that shall happen during the tribulation it is not the purpose here to try to explain what each means, but only to give an impression of the terrible conditions that shall exist upon earth during the day of wrath and vengeance of God, and in some measure show what those must experience who shall pass through that time. The post-tribulation view of the rapture holds that the Church of Christ shall pass through all these terrible judgments and woes. The pre-tribulation view holds that all believers will be raptured before these things come to pass, and thereby be delivered from the torment and agony thereof.

At the opening of the seventh seal are seen seven angels and each one is given a trumpet. Here are seven different trumpets which are to be sounded, each one bringing judgment upon the earth and those that dwell thereon.

"The first angel sounded, and there followed hail and fire mingled with blood, and they were cast upon the earth: and the third part of the trees was burnt up, and all green grass was burnt up" (8:7).

"And the second angel sounded, and as it were a great mountain burning with fire was cast into the sea: and the third part of the sea became blood; and the third part of the creatures which were in the sea, and had life, died; and the third part of the ships were destroyed" (vs. 8–9).

"And the third angel sounded, and there fell a great star from heaven, burning as it were a lamp, and it fell upon a third part of the rivers, and upon the fountains of waters: and the name of the star is called Wormwood: and the third part of the waters became wormwood; and many men died of the waters, because they were made bitter" (vs. 10–11).

"And the fourth angel sounded, and the third part of the sun was smitten, and the third part of the moon, and the third part of the stars; so as the third part of them was darkened, and the day shone not for a third part of it, and the night likewise. And I beheld, and heard an angel flying through the midst of heaven, saying with a loud voice, Woe, woe, woe, to the inhabiters of the earth by reason of the other voices of the trumpet of the three angels, which are yet to sound" (vs. 12–13).

"And the fifth angel sounded, and I saw a star fall from heaven unto the earth: and to him was given the key of the bottomless pit. And he opened the bottomless pit; and there arose a smoke out of the pit, as the smoke of a great furnace; and the sun and the air were darkened by reason of the smoke of the pit. And there came out of the smoke locusts upon the earth: and unto them was given power, as the scorpions of the earth have power. And it was commanded them that they should not hurt the grass of the earth, neither any green thing, neither any tree; but only those men which have not the seal of God in their foreheads. And to them was given that they should not kill them, but that they should be tormented five months: and their torment was as the torment of a scorpion, when he striketh a man. And in those days shall men seek death, and shall not find it; and shall desire to die, and death shall flee from them" (9:1–6).

"One woe is past; and, behold, there come two woes more hereafter" (v. 12).

"And the sixth angel sounded, and I heard a voice from the four horns of the golden altar which is before God, saying to the sixth angel which had the trumpet, Loose the four angels which are bound in the great river Euphrates. And the four angels were loosed, which were prepared for an hour, and a day, and a month, and a year, for to slay the third part of men. And the number of the army of the horsemen were two hundred thousand thousand: and I heard the number of them. By these three was the third part of men killed, by the fire, and by the smoke, and by the brimstone, which issued out of their mouths" (9:13–16, 18).

"And the same hour was there a great earthquake, and the tenth part of the city [Jerusalem] fell, and

in the earthquake were slain of men seven thousand.
. . . The second woe is past; and, behold, the third
woe cometh quickly" (11:13–14).

After the seventh trumpet, with its woe, had been
sounded, John saw Satan and his angels cast out of
heaven into the earth. Then he "heard a loud voice
saying. . . . Woe to the inhabiters of the earth and
of the sea! for the devil is come down unto you, having great wrath, because he knoweth that he hath
but a short time" (12:9, 12).

The tribulation reaches its greatest intensity as
seven angels pour upon the earth seven golden vials
(or bowls as in the American Standard Version)
filled with the wrath of God.

"And I heard a great voice out of the temple saying to the seven angels, Go your ways, and pour out
the vials of the wrath of God upon the earth.

"And the first went, and poured out his vial upon
the earth; and there fell a noisome and grievous sore
upon the men which had the mark of the beast, and
upon them which worshipped his image.

"And the second angel poured out his vial upon
the sea; and it became as the blood of a dead man:
and every living soul died in the sea.

"And the third angel poured out his vial upon the
rivers and fountains of waters; and they became
blood. . . .

"And the fourth angel poured out his vial upon
the sun; and power was given unto him to scorch
men with fire. And men were scorched with great
heat, and blasphemed the name of God, which hath

power over these plagues: and they repented not to give him glory.

"And the fifth angel poured out his vial upon the seat of the beast; and his kingdom was full of darkness; and they gnawed their tongues for pain, and blasphemed the God of heaven because of their pains and their sores, and repented not of their deeds.

"And the sixth angel poured out his vial upon the great river Euphrates; and the water thereof was dried up, that the way of the kings of the east might be prepared. And I saw three unclean spirits like frogs come out of the mouth of the dragon, and out of the mouth of the beast, and out of the mouth of the false prophet. For they are the spirits of devils, working miracles, which go forth unto the kings of the earth and of the whole world, to gather them to the battle of that great day of God Almighty . . . into a place called in the Hebrew tongue Armageddon.

"And the seventh angel poured out his vial into the air . . . and there was a great earthquake, such as was not since men were upon the earth. . . . And the great city was divided into three parts, and the cities of the nations fell. . . . And every island fled away, and the mountains were not found. And there fell upon men a great hail out of heaven, every stone about the weight of a talent: and men blasphemed God because of the plague of the hail; for the plague thereof was exceeding great" (16:1-21).

These things and much more that shall come to

pass during the tribulation are so awful that, as one has said: "It has seemed impossible to understand how they can be fulfilled, but now [when the atom bomb was exploded over Hiroshima] we do not see how they can be avoided." And yet as terrible as are the effects of the atom bomb, that which is prophesied to transpire during the tribulation shall be even worse for "in those days shall men seek death, and shall not find it; and shall desire to die, and death shall flee from them." Yes, God shall withhold death as a means of escape from the intense torment caused by His wrath.

This exercise of the wrath and fierce anger of God upon a God-rejecting mankind is the very opposite of His expression of grace and long-suffering in the present age. In grace is seen the infinite love of God toward the Church. Paul wrote: "For I am persuaded, that neither death, nor life, nor angels, nor principalities, nor powers, nor things present, nor things to come, nor height, nor depth, nor any other creature, shall be able to separate us from the love of God, which is in Christ Jesus" (Rom. 8:38–39).

A heavy responsibility rests upon those who hold the mid- and post-tribulation views to reconcile the claim that the Church will pass through these awful days of terror, or part of them, with Christ's love for her. They must also show good and valid reasons why the Church, for which Christ died that she might be saved from wrath, shall pass through that day of God's wrath. This responsibility seems to have been entirely overlooked.

CHAPTER 6

The Tribulation and the Day of the Lord

FROM the two preceding chapters it is evident that the tribulation and the day of the Lord have much in common. The purpose of this chapter is to show that the tribulation is the first several years of the day of the Lord.

A comparison of that which is said of the tribulation and of the early years of the day of the Lord will show beyond doubt that one and the same period of time is described. The importance of this is that when Paul wrote to the Thessalonian saints of the rapture of the Church he related that event to the coming of the day of the Lord (1 Thess. 4:15—5:3). As the purpose of this study is to show that the Church will not pass through the tribulation it must be shown that the coming of the day of the Lord is the same as the coming of the tribulation.

Describing the day of the Lord, Joel prophesied: "There hath not been ever the like, neither shall be any more after it" (Joel 2:2b); and Jesus said: "For then shall be great tribulation, such as was not since the beginning of the world to this time, no, nor ever shall be. And except those days should be shortened, there should no flesh be saved" (Matt. 24:21–22). These two statements must refer to the same period of time. That much of chapters 6–19 of Revelation is descriptive of that time of unprecedented tribulation cannot be questioned.

At the very beginning of the tribulation, when the Lamb began to exercise His power in judgment by opening the first seal, John saw a rider on a white horse that brought a period of peace. This peace was suddenly broken by a rider on a red horse. The third and fourth horsemen added to the destruction caused by the second one. Paul said the coming of the day of the Lord shall be at a time "when they shall say, Peace and safety." Then sudden destruction shall come from which they shall not escape.

The rider on the black horse that John saw when the third seal was opened stands for famine. The fourth horseman is also given power to kill with hunger. Joel, in his first reference to the day of the Lord, said: "Is not the meat cut off before our eyes, yea, joy and gladness from the house of our God? The seed is rotten under their clods, the garners are laid desolate, the barns are broken down; for the corn is withered. How do the beasts groan! the herds of cattle are perplexed, because they have no pasture; yea, the flocks of sheep are made desolate" (1:16–18). This is a picture of great famine, apparently at the beginning of the day of the Lord, just as famine is seen during the early part of the tribulation.

To the rider on the pale horse was given power over one-fourth part of the earth to kill with sword and with hunger and with the beasts of the earth (6:8). Of the day of the Lord Isaiah said: "For by fire and by his sword will the LORD plead with all flesh: and the slain of the LORD shall be many" (Isa. 66:16).

With the opening of the sixth seal is seen much that the Old Testament prophets ascribe to the day of the Lord. John wrote: "And I beheld when he had opened the sixth seal, and, lo, there was a great earthquake; and the sun became black as sackcloth of hair, and the moon became as blood; and the stars of heaven fell unto the earth. . . . And the heaven departed as a scroll when it is rolled together; and every mountain and island were moved out of their places" (Rev. 6:12–14).

Compare with the above the following quotations from the prophets describing the day of the Lord: "I will shake the heavens, and the earth shall move out of her place" (Isa. 13:13); "The heavens and the earth shall shake" (Joel 3:16); "For the stars of heaven and the constellations thereof shall not give their light: the sun shall be darkened in his going forth, and the moon shall not cause her light to shine" (Isa. 13:10); "And all the hosts of heaven shall be dissolved, and the heavens shall be rolled together as a scroll" (Isa. 34:4); "And I will shew wonders in the heavens and in the earth, blood, and fire, and pillars of smoke. The sun shall be turned into darkness, and the moon into blood, before the great and the terrible day of the LORD come" (Joel 2:30–31).

There can be no mistake in concluding that these demonstrations of the terror of God at the opening

THE TRIBULATION AND THE DAY OF THE LORD

of the sixth seal belong to the day of the Lord; but more, the effects upon the inhabitants of the world are the same as foretold for the day of the Lord. "And the kings of the earth, and the great men, and the rich men, and the chief captains, and the mighty men, and every bondman, and every free man, hid themselves in the dens and in the rocks of the mountains; and said to the mountains and rocks, Fall on us, and hide us from the face of him that sitteth on the throne, and from the wrath of the Lamb" (Rev. 6:15–16). Of the day of the Lord Isaiah wrote: "And they shall go into the holes of the rocks, and into the caves of the earth, for fear of the LORD, and for the glory of his majesty, when he ariseth to shake terribly the earth" (2:19).

It is again important to emphasize the fact that the day of the Lord is the day of His wrath. So also is the tribulation. That is the only explanation of the terrible things that come to pass at that time. It is the wrath and fierce anger of God that sets this period apart from all other days and gives to it its characteristics.

The description of the results of the breaking of the sixth seal closes with these supremely important words: "For the great day of his wrath is come; and who shall be able to stand" (Rev. 6:17). Yes, the tribulation is the day of His wrath. So also Isaiah described the day of the Lord: "Behold, the day of the LORD cometh, cruel both with wrath and fierce anger" (13:9). Zephaniah also identified wrath with that day: "That day is a day of wrath" (Zeph. 1:15).

The use by Joel, in Chapter 2:31, of the term "the great and the terrible day of the LORD," after having twice used the customary name "the day of the LORD," indicates a special period of intensified terror and wrath of God. This same emphasis is seen in the expression, "the great day of his wrath," found in Revelation 6:17.

This period, known as "the day of the Lord," "a time of trouble," "great tribulation," and "the hour of temptation which shall come upon all the world," is also called "the day of Jacob's trouble." "For thus saith the LORD; We have heard a voice of trembling, of fear, and not of peace. Ask ye now, and see whether a man doth travail with child? wherefore do I see every man with his hands on his loins, as a woman in travail, and all faces are turned into paleness? Alas! for that day is great, so that none is like it: it is even the day of Jacob's trouble, but he shall be saved out of it" (Jer. 30:5–7). The words, "Alas! for that day is great, so that none is like it," clearly identify that day with both the tribulation and the day of the Lord.

When Paul wrote, "For yourselves know perfectly that the day of the Lord so cometh as a thief in the night" (1 Thess. 5:2), he could have written, For yourselves know perfectly that the tribulation so cometh as a thief in the night. It would have had exactly the same meaning. Why did he not do so? For those living now it would have been more readily understood. The very good reason was that the Revelation was not written by John until some forty years later. Also, the Church at Thessalonica had within its membership Jews well versed in the writings of the Old Testament prophets which describe the day of the Lord.

When does the day of the Lord begin? It is important to know just when the day of the Lord shall begin. John was given a vision of a scene in heaven which must be the opening event of the day of the Lord.

"I saw in the right hand of him that sat on the throne a book written within and on the backside, sealed with seven seals. . . . And no man in heaven, nor in earth, neither under the earth, was able to open the book, neither to look thereon. And I wept much because no man was found worthy to open and to read the book, neither to look thereon. And one of the elders saith unto me, Weep not: behold, the Lion of the tribe of Juda, the Root of David, hath prevailed to open the book, and to loose the seven seals thereof. And I beheld, and, lo, in the midst of the throne and of the four beasts, and in the midst of the elders, stood a Lamb as it had been slain. . . . And he came and took the book out of the right hand of him that sat upon the throne" (Rev. 5:1, 3–7). Here is seen One to whom is given power far greater than that of any man. Here the Lion of the tribe of Judah, the root of David, is seen receiving His power to execute judgment and to rule as King of kings and Lord of lords.

He is also seen as "a Lamb as it had been slain." He is the One of whom John the Baptist said: "Behold the Lamb of God, which taketh away the sin of the world" (John 1:29). When He, on the cross, was slain, He took away sin by giving His own precious blood to redeem men from sin and the penalty thereof. When He shall take the seven-sealed book and open the seals thereof He shall again take away sin from the earth. Then it will not be in grace as the first time, but in wrath will He destroy the sinners, and thoroughly purge the earth. He, and He alone, is worthy to do that because He provided by His life blood the means of escape.

The seven-sealed book has remained sealed during the day of grace, during the long-suffering of God. When the first seal is opened the day of grace will have come to an end and the day of God's wrath and fierce anger will be at hand.

"When he had taken the book, the four living creatures and the four and twenty elders fell down before the Lamb. . . . And they sing a new song saying, Worthy art thou to take the book, and to open the seals thereof: for thou wast slain, and didst purchase unto God with thy blood men of every tribe, and tongue, and people, and nation, and madest them to be unto our God a kingdom and priests; and they reign upon the earth" (Rev. 5:8–10, A.S.V.).

"And I saw, and I heard a voice of many angels round about the throne and the living creatures and the elders; . . . saying with a great voice, Worthy is the Lamb that hath been slain to receive the power, and riches, and wisdom, and might, and honor, and glory, and blessing" (vs. 11–12, A.S.V.).

And every created being in heaven, on earth, and under the earth was heard saying, "Unto him that sitteth on the throne, and unto the Lamb, be the blessing, and the honor, and the glory, and the dominion, for ever and ever" (v. 13, A.S.V.).

Surely this scene in heaven must depict the opening event of the day of the Lord. Here are power, riches, wisdom, might, honor, glory, blessing, and dominion ascribed to the Lamb, all of which He will exercise during His day, the day of the Lord. This is His inauguration day.

The Lamb begins to exercise His power to judge the dwellers on the earth when He opens the first seal. This is His first recorded official act. The day of the Lord has then begun. The going forth of the rider on the white horse to conquer in peace must be the time of which Paul wrote: "The day of the Lord so cometh as a thief in the night . . . when they shall say, Peace and safety." The going forth of the rider on the red horse, when the second seal is opened, is the sudden destruction from which "they shall not escape." It is to this coming of the day of the Lord that Paul relates the rapture. See Chapter 10. The pre-tribulation view places the rapture at this time. Evidence in support of this view will be given in later chapters.

Joel prophesied: "The sun shall be turned into darkness, and the moon into blood, before the great and terrible day of the LORD come" (2:31). This is evidently the same as that which John saw when the

Lamb "opened the sixth seal . . . the sun became black as sackcloth of hair, and the moon became as blood" (Rev. 6:12). It is of this time that it is said, "For the great day of his [the Lamb's] wrath is come" (v. 17). It is important to notice that in the above verse Joel used the words "the great and terrible day of the LORD." Earlier in his prophecy he twice used the simple expression "day of the LORD" without any modifying words. As the divine Author of the Bible has been very exact in the use of words, this passage must refer to a limited period of special terror and wrath during the day of the Lord. No indication is given of the duration of this period but because the judgments and wrath of the last three and a half years of the tribulation will be of great intensity it is possible that "the great and terrible day of the LORD" corresponds to that time. The mid-tribulation view places the rapture just before the last three and a half years of the tribulation.

The millennial reign of Christ belongs to the day of the Lord. In fact it is the essential part and purpose thereof. The destruction with which the day of the Lord will come and the wrath of that day is a short period of purging the earth and the human race in preparation for the glorious reign of Christ. This important and major aspect of the day of the Lord will begin when the Son of man shall come in the clouds of heaven with power and great glory to reign on the earth. It is at this time that post-tribulationists place the rapture. Evidence will be given to show that this view is unscriptural.

CHAPTER 7

The Church Age and Seventieth Week
of Israel

THE Bible tells of a future period of time, well defined in its duration, as regards that which is to be accomplished therein, and concerning its time in God's program. It is commonly called the seventieth week of Daniel, but, as has been suggested, the seventieth week of Israel is more to the point.

It was revealed to Daniel that seventy weeks were determined upon his people and his holy city "to finish the transgression, and to make an end of sins, and to make reconciliation [atonement, A.S.V.] for iniquity, and to bring in everlasting righteousness, and to seal up the vision and prophecy, and to anoint the most Holy" (Dan. 9:24). This revelation to Daniel is of great significance in the study of future events.

This is a fixed period of time. It is also a period during which God deals with His earthly people, Israel. The transgressions of Israel are to be finished, their sins are to come to an end, and atonement shall be made for their iniquities. At the end of these seventy weeks, visions and prophecy shall have been fulfilled, righteousness shall be brought in, and the Most Holy shall be anointed.

During the early part of the sixty-nine weeks
(seven and sixty-two) Jerusalem was rebuilt in trou-
blous times. All of these sixty-nine weeks had run
their course when Israel's Messiah was cut off (v. 26).
The elapsed time from the decree by Artaxerxes to
rebuild Jerusalem (Neh. 2:8) until the crucifixion
of Jesus is proof that each week is a period of seven
years.

At the end of the sixty-ninth week a sudden break
came in this time determined upon Israel. With this
break in the seventy weeks began an interim period
which has already lasted more than nineteen hundred years. During this time the city of Jerusalem
has again been destroyed and war and desolation
have been the order of events. For that period Jesus
foretold "wars and rumours of wars" (Matt. 24:6).

But something else, not revealed to Daniel or any
Old Testament prophet, was in God's purpose for
this interim period. The calling out of the Church,
the body and bride of Christ, was in that purpose.

During the sixty-nine weeks, and for centuries before, God had made a difference between Israel and
the Gentile nations. He had commanded absolute
separation. The Gentiles were "aliens from the com-
monwealth of Israel, and strangers from the cove-
nants of promise having no hope, and without God
in the world" (Eph. 2:12). When the sixty-ninth
week came to a close God took away completely the
difference between the Jew and the Gentile. Both
were declared to be under sin (Rom. 3:9). Both are
offered the righteousness of God on the one condi-

tion of faith (Rom. 3:22). Both are made into one new man in Christ. Both are reconciled unto God in one body by the cross (Eph. 2:15–16). In calling out the Church God disregards all distinctions between Jew and Gentile. But when the seventieth week shall commence this distinction shall again be seen.

At Pentecost, immediately after the end of the sixty-ninth week, the Holy Spirit came to earth in a way He had never come before, to begin the work of taking out of the world and perfecting the Church for her heavenly destiny. This work of the Holy Spirit has continued for more than nineteen hundred years and will continue until He returns to heaven with the Church, at the end of the interim period, before the wicked one can be revealed. See Chapter 11.

It is of the greatest importance to recognize the difference between the Church and Israel. Both worship the One and only true and living God but the Church has a heavenly, while Israel has an earthly, calling. The two must not be confused. Christianity, the Church, does not come out of Judaism, Israel, as some think. Christianity is a new thing, entirely distinct from Judaism. The Church is a new creation in Christ (2 Cor. 5:17). Every member of the Church is born of God (John 1:13), is born of the Spirit (John 3:5), and of incorruptible seed by the Word of God (1 Peter 1:23), and has a divine nature. Every member has been identified with Christ in death (Rom. 6:4) and in resurrection

(Col. 3:1), and is seated in Him in the heavenlies (Eph. 2:6).

Every member of Israel is nothing more than of the human seed of Abraham and has no promise for the future greater than being given a new heart with the desire to serve God fully.

The promised blessings for the Church are spiritual and heavenly (Eph. 1:3, A.S.V.). All blessings promised Israel are earthly, are centered in Palestine, and are conditioned upon obedience to God (Deut. 28:1–14).

God's future purpose with the Church is also vastly different from that for Israel. The Church shall forever be with the Lord (1 Thess. 4:17), to behold His glory (John 17:24). Every member of the Church shall be like Him (1 John 3:2). "For the . . . Lord Jesus Christ . . . shall change our vile body, that it may be fashioned like unto his glorious body" (Phil. 3:20–21). The Church has been called "to the obtaining of the glory of our Lord Jesus Christ" (2 Thess. 2:14).

God's purpose with Israel was to declare to mankind that He only is God (Isa. 42:11–12). He purposed that all nations of the earth shall be blessed through Israel. He said to Abraham: "And in thy seed [i.e., Israel] shall all nations of the earth be blessed" (Gen. 13:15–16; 22:18). This promise was confirmed to Isaac (Gen. 26:4) and again to Jacob (Gen. 28:14). In these promises are always found the words "of the earth." This shows that God's purpose for Israel is earthly.

Here are two separate and distinct programs. That for Israel was interrupted at the close of the sixty-ninth week because Israel rejected and crucified her Messiah through whom that program should have been fulfilled.

Then God immediately began His program for the Church. He will carry it to completion in the rapture of the Church. When that has been accomplished He will return to purify and prepare Israel to accept their Messiah by whom God's program for them shall be carried out.

The seventieth week of Israel will witness this purification of Israel. No such purifying process is needed by the Church. She has been "sanctified through the offering of the body of Jesus Christ once for all." By this offering He "hath perfected for ever them that are sanctified" (Heb. 10:10, 14).

But not all Israel will suffer under the rod. During the tribulation will be seen a faithful remnant of twelve thousand from each of the twelve tribes of Israel, sealed in their foreheads with the seal of God. This is evidence that God will then use Israel once more to carry out His purpose on earth. As long as the Church is on earth there are no saved Israelites as such. In the Church there is no distinction between Jews and Gentiles. But during the tribulation, which is also the seventieth week, this distinction reappears in these 144,000 of the twelve tribes of Israel. Here is evidence that God's program for the Church on earth will then have been completed. The seventieth week of Israel will then have begun.

Because no other group is seen to witness for God during the tribulation it is evident that the seventieth week runs its course during that time.

Although more than nineteen hundred years have already separated the seventieth week from the other sixty-nine, that week is still a part of the seventy weeks determined upon Israel.

The beginning of the week will be signalized by a covenant made with Israel by a ruler who is called the prince of the people that destroyed Jerusalem (Dan. 9:27). As Jerusalem was destroyed by the Roman armies, it has been held that the prince here spoken of shall be the ruler of a revived Roman empire. In view of the present Arab influence this "prince" shall be one of great and widespread power in order to covenant with Israel to re-establish their worship in Jerusalem.

It is significant that at the opening of the first seal a rider on a white horse will be given a crown and "he went forth conquering, and to conquer" (Rev. 6:2). This person also must be a great ruler. As the end time shall witness but one world dictator, these two references speak of the same person.

When the covenant is signed with Israel and when the rider on the white horse goes forth with a bow, but no arrows, there is an apparent period of peace but at best it is a time of false security because the covenant is quickly broken and the rider on the white horse is followed by war. This period of false security has already been seen at the coming of the day of the Lord and will be seen again in these studies.

The seventieth week will have come to its end when everlasting righteousness shall be brought in and the Most Holy shall be anointed. This will be accomplished when the Son of man shall come in the clouds of heaven with power and great glory.

The end of the seventieth week must, then, coincide with the end of the tribulation. This is reasonable assurance that the full tribulation period will have a duration of approximately, if not exactly, seven years.

Jesus identified the seventieth week with the tribulation. He said that when the abomination of desolation spoken of by Daniel (Dan. 9:27) shall stand in the holy place there shall be great tribulation, such as was not since the world began, nor ever shall be (Matt. 24:15, 21).

The seventieth week is important because God will then again work out His purpose on earth through Israel and because it coincides with the full duration of the tribulation.

During the period between the sixty-ninth and seventieth weeks God has set Israel aside. Through the Church, empowered by the Holy Spirit, He has been calling mankind unto Himself. This ministry did not commence until the sixty-ninth week was completed. No evidence can be found to show that it will continue after the seventieth week begins, nor that any will then be added to the Church. No reason can be found for the Church remaining on earth after the Church age has come to an end.

On the contrary, God's Word declares that His work of perfecting the Church shall be finished before He again turns to Israel. In the council at Jerusalem James said: "Simeon hath declared how God at first did visit the Gentiles, to take out of them a people for his name. And to this agree the words of the prophets; as it is written, After this I will return, and build again the tabernacle of David" (Acts 15: 13–16). It is *after* God has taken out "a people for his name," the Church, that He shall return to Israel to rebuild the tabernacle of David. The work of taking out the Church will not be completed until it has been caught up to meet the Lord in the air. The rapture must, therefore, precede the beginning of the seventieth week, the time when God shall again turn to Israel. As this will also be the beginning of the tribulation, the rapture must come before that period begins.

There is also evidence that the Church will be fully perfected before God begins to deal with the Christ-rejecting world. The Church, as already mentioned, is called by the gospel of grace "to the obtaining of the glory of our Lord Jesus Christ" (2 Thess. 2:14). The last act, then, in perfecting the Church must be to bring her into glory.

Paul declared that the long-suffering of God with the wicked world is in order that He might show the riches of His glory on those whom He has prepared unto glory, that is, the Church. "What if God, willing to shew his wrath, and to make his power known, endured with much longsuffering the vessels of wrath fitted for destruction: and that he might make known the riches of his glory on the vessels of mercy, which he had afore prepared unto glory, even us, whom he hath called, not of Jews only, but also of the Gentiles?" (Rom. 9:22–24).

God in the present age is preparing the Church unto glory but will not have shown the *riches* of His glory until He has brought her into glory by the rapture. Until then His long-suffering, the day of grace, will continue. When that shall be done His long-suffering comes to an end and He shall show His power and wrath and bring destruction upon those who are fitted thereto. Not before then shall the day of His power and wrath, the day of the Lord, begin.

This, again, shows beyond a doubt that the Church will be raptured before the tribulation begins because the Lamb begins to show His power when the first seal is broken.

Here is strong evidence that the Church will not go through the tribulation.

CHAPTER 8

The Parousia of the Son of Man and
the Lord Jesus Christ

THE Greek word *parousia* (pronounced pȧ-roo'-zhĭ-*a*) has entered into the discussion of the time of the rapture to a marked degree. Both pre- and post-tribulationists have used it to advance their respective views. Usually the discussion of any word of an ancient language is more or less bewildering to the average reader and not a little tiring. Often it is impossible to follow such a discussion. Fortunately that need not be true of the word *parousia* for with the use of Young's Analytical Concordance and a good dictionary of Greek New Testament words even one entirely unlearned in the Greek language of Bible times can satisfactorily pursue the study of this word.

No word in the English language carries the full meaning of the Greek word *parousia*. The English word *coming* does not fully express the meaning of the coming of the Lord as does this word. Therefore, the study of this word is of great importance and *the verses containing this word become the outstanding passages* in determining whether the coming of the Lord shall be before or after the tribulation.

According to Young, *parousia* occurs twenty-four times in the New Testament. Twice it is translated by the English word *presence* and twenty-two times by *coming*.

The word has been explained as denoting "both an arrival and a subsequent presence with." For instance, in a papyrus letter a lady speaks of the necessity of her parousia in a place in order to attend to matters relating to her property there (Vine).

The Apostle Paul in his letters twice referred to his parousia in the sense of his presence. He wrote to the Corinthians: "For his letters, say they, are weighty and powerful; but his bodily presence [parousia] is weak, and his speech contemptible" (2 Cor. 10:10). To the Philippians he wrote: "Beloved, as ye have always obeyed, not as in my presence [parousia] only, but now much more in my absence" (Phil. 2:12).

In all three of the above citations the presence is the important aspect of the word.

One post-tribulation writer treats the word *parousia* as having the limited meaning of a sovereign coming to visit his subjects and then represents the parousia of the Lord as being His coming to reign. The Lord's coming is called "the *parousia* of the King." The fact is that there is not a single passage in the Bible in which the word *parousia* is related to the Kingship of Christ. It is the parousia of the Son of man, of the Lord Jesus Christ, and of the Lord, but never of the King. In the passage which tells of His coming in the clouds of heaven with power and great glory this word is not used. It is always well to adhere closely to the exact expressions of the Bible and not add anything from the outside.

Now turning to the consideration of the twenty-two times that parousia is translated *coming,* it is used four times of the coming of men. Paul wrote: "I am glad of the coming [parousia] of Stephanas and Fortunatus and Achaicus: for that which was lacking on your part they have supplied" (1 Cor. 16:17). "Nevertheless God . . . comforted us by the coming [parousia] of Titus; and not by his coming [parousia] only, but by the consolation wherewith he was comforted in you" (2 Cor. 7:6–7). "That your rejoicing may be more abundant in Jesus Christ for me by my coming [parousia] to you again" (Phil. 1:26).

In all four of these instances the word is used to denote the arrival of some person or persons, but it is more than that. It was the subsequent presence that brought the blessing. If the mere arrival had been all, then some other word would have been used. Here again is also proof that the word was of common usage and not limited to the coming of rulers.

Of the remaining eighteen times the word *parousia* is used, one is in connection with the wicked one: "whose coming [parousia] is after the working of Satan with all power and signs and lying wonders" (2 Thess. 2:9). Here also an arrival with a subsequent presence is in view.

Another use of this word is by Peter where he speaks of the coming of the Lord Jesus Christ on the Mount of Transfiguration (2 Pet. 1:16–17).

Still another time it is used in connection with the coming of the day of God which is after the thousand-year reign of Christ (2 Pet. 3:12). Once it is used by the disciples of Jesus when, on Mount Olivet, they asked him what would be the sign of His coming (Matt. 24:3), and once it is used by scoffers who ask: "Where is the promise of his coming?" (2 Pet. 3:4).

Three times Jesus used the word concerning His own coming as the Son of man and ten times it is used of the coming of the Lord and of the Lord Jesus Christ.

The three times that Jesus spoke of His parousia are found in the twenty-fourth chapter of Matthew. Other verses, as for example Matthew 24:30, in which the coming of the Son of man is mentioned, do not contain the word *parousia* but some other word with a lesser meaning. Hence, for the study of the parousia of the Son of man only three passages can be considered.

It is important to recognize that the parousia of the Son of man has in view His coming to deal with conditions on the earth while the parousia of the Lord Jesus Christ is not spoken of in relation to things to happen on earth, but in relation to the Church. The parousia of the Lord is in relation to both the Church and the day of the Lord. The parousia of the Son of man is for judgment upon the inhabitants of the world, both Israel and the Gentiles. The first time the Son of man came to the earth He came "to minister, and to give his life a ransom for many" (Matt. 20:28). He "came not to judge the world, but to save the world" (John 12:47). At His parousia He will come to judge, for all judgment is committed unto Him (John 5:22). He is given authority to execute judgment because He is the Son of man (John 5:27). To those who have heard His words and believed on Him who sent Him He cannot come as the Son of man to judge, because they shall not come into judgment (John 5:24, A.S.V.).

To Israel He is the Son of man because to them He is the Son of David and the Seed of Abraham (Gal. 3:16). Only so can He rule over that nation, and fulfill the prophecies. He must also come as the Son of man for they shall see Him whom they pierced and that was the Son of man.

But to the Church—the new creation in Christ— He is the Lord Jesus Christ. He is not the Son of man, as Paul wrote: "Yea, though we have known Christ after the flesh, yet now henceforth know we him no more" (2 Cor. 5:16).

In all passages referring to the parousia of the Son of man is seen judgment and carnage. In Matthew 24:37–39 are these words of Jesus: "But as the days of Noe were, so shall also the coming [parousia] of the Son of man be. For as in the days that were before the flood they were eating and drinking, marrying and giving in marriage, until the day that Noe entered into the ark, and knew not until the flood came, and took them all away; so shall also the coming [parousia] of the Son of man be." Here again is seen that period of false security followed by destruction which has already been seen at the beginning of the seventieth week of Israel and also at the beginning of the tribulation. It is the time "when they shall say, Peace and safety" followed by sudden destruction at the coming of the day of the Lord.

"They were eating and drinking, marrying and giving in marriage." These words describe a normal condition of life from the earliest days of the human race. They have the same meaning as the words of the scoffers of whom Peter wrote, who said: "Where is the promise of his coming? for since the fathers fell asleep, all things continue as they were from the beginning of creation" (2 Pet. 3:4).

These words describe conditions on the earth at the parousia of the Son of man. Things shall be as from the beginning when God commanded Adam and Eve to "be fruitful, and multiply, and replenish the earth." Such a time cannot possibly be found at any time during the tribulation, of which Jesus said: "Such as was not since the beginning of this world to this time, no, nor ever shall be" (Matt. 24:21). There can be no complacency nor unexpected destruction after the most terrible destruction of all time has begun. Nor can this destruction come when the Son of man shall come in the clouds of heaven. He shall then come to restore and establish peace on earth. *Yes, this must be before the tribulation begins.*

But it is at just such a period of false security that the parousia of the Son of man shall be. The coming of the Son of man *must*, then, be before there shall be any indications to the world of the coming destruction, of the tribulation period.

Luke in his record of the same discourse used somewhat different words which make it even more clear that after the arrival aspect of the parousia there shall be a period of time, probably short, when the peoples of the earth shall continue to live normal lives, unmindful of the impending destruction. "And as it was in the days of Noe, so shall it be also in the days of the Son of man. They did eat, they drank, they married wives, they were given in marriage, until the day that Noe entered into the ark, and the flood came, and destroyed them all. Likewise also as it was in the days of Lot; they did eat, they drank, they bought, they sold, they planted, they builded; but the same day that Lot went out of Sodom it rained fire and brimstone from heaven and destroyed them all" (Luke 17:26–29). Here again, the destruction came at a time when it was not expected. When Lot warned his "sons in law" to get out of Sodom, "he seemed as one that mocked" unto them (Gen. 19:14). Such a period can come *only before* the judgments of the tribulation begin.

Luke's phrase, "in the days of the Son of man" is descriptive of a period of time, not a momentary event. These words express the same idea as the words "the coming [parousia] of the Son of man," used by Matthew. This shows clearly that the parousia is not only an arrival, but a subsequent presence with.

The other reference to the parousia of the Son of man is found in Matthew 24:27: "For as the lightning cometh out of the east, and shineth even unto the west; so shall also the coming [parousia] of the Son of man be." According to a footnote in the American Standard (Revised) Version, an alternate translation would read: "so shall also the presence of the Son of man be." This is followed by the description of a great carnage. "For wheresoever the carcase is, there will the eagles [vultures] be gathered together." Here then the parousia is seen as being related to the carnage *during* the tribulation.

That which is here in view is undoubtedly later than the arrival aspect of the parousia as in the days of Noah in verses 37–39. Beginning with verse 22 Jesus explained how it can be known when the parousia of the Son of man will be near. Therefore, verses 37–39 do not follow chronologically verse 27. A comparison of the order in Luke 17:26–31 with Matthew 24:16–18, 37–39 confirms this view.

The question may be asked, What is there to hinder a parousia at the beginning of the tribulation and another at or near the end? The answer to this is that the disciples' question (v. 3) indicates that they knew of but one. Furthermore all three times that Jesus used the word *parousia* it was in the singular and each time the definite article was used. Thus it is clear that Jesus spoke about only one parousia. This being so, one is led to the conclusion that verses 37–39 tell of the arrival and verse 27 of some event during the subsequent presence.

Luke's version of Matthew 24:27 clearly indicates that this reference to the parousia is to a period of time rather than to an arrival. "For as the lightning, that lighteneth out of the one part under heaven, shineth unto the other part under heaven; so shall also the Son of man be in his day" (Luke 17:24). As already mentioned, the word *day* always means a period of time. Here it evidently means that period of time during which the Son of man will pour His judgments upon the dwellers on the earth.

It is not until after the tribulation of those days which have brought about the great carnage that the sign of the Son of man shall appear in heaven. Then shall all the tribes of the earth see the Son of man coming in the clouds of heaven with power and great glory. Notice the emphasis here is on the appearing of the sign of the Son of man and that all tribes of the earth shall see Him. This coming of the Son of man is not said to be the parousia.

Inasmuch as parousia denotes not only an arrival but also a subsequent presence with, these three occurrences of the parousia of the Son of man teach that at His arrival the judgments of God, as seen in the sudden destruction, commence. During the subsequent presence, He shall mete out judgments, but does not reveal Himself in power and glory to the tribes of the earth until after the tribulation.

Of the remaining ten passages, which refer to the parousia of the Lord Jesus Christ, six give no indication of the time of that event, and therefore need no examination here. These are: 1 Thessalonians

2:19; 3:13; 5:23; James 5:7–8; 1 John 2:28. The remaining four bear careful study.

One of the most illuminating of these four is found in 1 Thessalonians 4:15–17: "For this we say unto you by the word of the Lord, that we which are alive and remain unto the coming [parousia] of the Lord shall not prevent [precede, A.S.V.] them which are asleep. For the Lord himself shall descend from heaven with a shout, with the voice of the archangel, and with the trump of God: and the dead in Christ shall rise first: then we which are alive and remain shall be caught up together with them in the clouds, to meet the Lord in the air." This passage clearly speaks of the arrival aspect of the parousia. The shout, the voice of the archangel, and the trump of God strongly suggest that when the Lord Himself descends from heaven He will come on three great and distinct missions.

The shout will raise the dead in Christ. They shall then hear the voice of the Son of God and come forth from their graves (John 5:28–29), just as Lazarus did when Jesus cried with a loud voice, "Lazarus come forth" (John 11:43). In the same twinkling of an eye that the dead in Christ are raised the Church shall be raptured.

The voice of the archangel must be for Israel because Michael, the archangel, is the great prince that stands for Israel. When he stands up "there shall be a time of trouble, such as never was since there was a nation" (Dan. 12:1). Notice carefully that the archangel will stand up before the time of unprecedented trouble begins. This suggests the beginning of the seventieth week of Israel, and God's call to them again to carry out His purpose on earth.

Isaiah foretold that the Lord would blow a trumpet for the dwellers on the earth: "All ye inhabitants of the world, and dwellers on the earth, see ye, when he lifteth up an ensign on the mountains; and when he bloweth a trumpet, hear ye" (Isa. 18:3). This suggests that the trump of God, with which the Lord descends from heaven, is for the dwellers on the earth. Isaiah sheds more light on the threefold mission upon which the Lord shall come at His parousia. "For, behold, the LORD cometh out of his place to punish the inhabitants of the earth for their iniquity" (Isa. 26:21). This is in harmony with the parousia of the Son of man to bring sudden destruction upon the dwellers on the earth. Zephaniah confirms the thought that the trump is for the day of the Lord. He declared that the day of the Lord is "a day of the trumpet and alarm against the fenced cities; and against the high towers" at a time the Lord will bring distress upon men (1:16–17).

Post-tribulationists correctly hold that no separation should have been made between 1 Thessalonians 4 and 5. That being true the coming of the day of the Lord, as described in 5:2–3, is also related to the parousia just as is the raising of the dead and the rapture of the Church. Because of the order in which Paul was inspired to describe these two events the *coming* of the day of the Lord will be at the same time or immediately following the rapture. In other words the rapture will precede the day of the Lord.

The day of the Lord comes with sudden destruction at a time when they shall say "Peace and safety." As has already been explained no such time can possibly come except at the beginning of the tribulation. No period of peace and safety can be found during the tribulation because from the time of the going forth of the second rider, the one on the red horse, there will be no peace on earth until the Prince of Peace shall come. Then the time of destruction will be in the past.

At the parousia, then, the Lord descends from heaven not only to rapture the Church but to bring in the day of the Lord with its destruction upon His enemies. He shall then, as Isaiah said, go forth from His place, which is heaven, to punish His enemies.

Here is both Old and New Testament evidence that the parousia shall be before the tribulation begins.

Because the rapture of the Church will be an instantaneous event at the time the Lord descends from heaven, it *must* precede the beginning of the tribulation.

The statement by James, previously quoted, that God shall return to Israel after having taken out of the Gentiles a people for His name, confirms the above conclusion. So also does the statement by Paul that God shall endure with much long-suffering the vessels of wrath until He has made known the riches of His glory on the Church. See Chapter 7.

Additional proof that the Church shall, by the

rapture, escape the wrath of the day of the Lord will be found in Chapter 10.

In the second letter to the Thessalonians Paul again spoke of the parousia. "Now we beseech you, brethren, touching the coming [parousia] of our Lord Jesus Christ, and our gathering together unto him" (2:1, A.S.V.). Here again the parousia and the rapture are seen to be at the same time. In Chapter 11 of this study it is shown that the rapture of the Church must be before the tribulation because the Holy Spirit, who indwells the believer and abides forever, must be taken out of the way before the man of sin can be revealed and that time begin. It again follows that the parousia also must precede the tribulation.

From the above it is seen that the Lord Jesus Christ will come again for the Church at the same time that He as the Son of man will come to bring judgment upon the dwellers of the earth. The one is the heavenly aspect, and the other the earthly aspect of the same great event.

In concluding this chapter there is one more important passage to be considered, namely, 1 Corinthians 15:22–23: "For as in Adam all die, even so in Christ shall all be made alive. But every man in his own order: Christ the first-fruits; afterward they that are Christ's at his coming" [parousia]. This passage clearly states that they that are Christ's shall be made alive at His parousia. This is in harmony with 1 Thessalonians 4:15–16 which has already been shown to teach that the parousia, the resurrection of the dead in Christ, and the rapture shall all be before the tribulation begins.

One passage remains, 2 Thessalonians 2:8. While this refers to the parousia, it tells only of a single aspect thereof. For that reason it is reserved for special consideration in the next chapter.

Even at the risk of becoming a bit tiresome this study covers every occurrence of the word *parousia* so as to eliminate any possible charge that some difficult use thereof has been omitted. This word is *never* used to tell of an arrival of either the Lord Jesus Christ or of the Son of man after the tribulation. It is always before that time shall begin. In the sense of a subsequent presence exercising an influence over the dwellers of the earth it is seen during the awful carnage of those days.

The use of the word *parousia* proves a pre-tribulation coming of the Lord and the rapture of the Church.

CHAPTER 9

The Manifestation of the Parousia

O NE of the important passages which throws light
on the time of the parousia in relation to the
tribulation is 2 Thessalonians 2:8. "And then shall
be revealed the lawless one, whom the Lord Jesus
shall slay with the breath of his mouth, and bring
to nought by the manifestation of his coming"
(parousia, A.S.V.). Here again the American Standard (Revised) Version gives *presence* as an alternate
translation of *parousia.* In the Authorized Version
the last phrase reads: "shall destroy with the brightness of his coming."

Because the lawless one shall be destroyed at the
end of the tribulation, this verse has been held to
support the view that the parousia, followed by the
rapture, shall come after the tribulation.

It was shown in the preceding chapter that, according to Matthew 24:37–39, the parousia of the
Son of man shall bring sudden destruction upon an
unsuspecting world. This, as has already been explained, unquestionably places the parousia, in the
sense of an arrival, before the tribulation begins.

By insisting that the destruction of the wicked one
places the parousia at the end of the tribulation, the
post-tribulationist must choose between three alternatives. First, Paul, in 2 Thessalonians 2:8, contra-

dicts the words of Jesus in Matthew 24:37–39. This, of course, is unthinkable. Second, there will be two arrivals, one before and one after the tribulation. This has been violently denied by post-tribulation-ists. Third, the parousia, in the sense of an arrival, shall be before the tribulation begins, and in the sense of a subsequent presence shall continue through the tribulation. This, too, is destructive to the post-tribulation view. One ardent post-tribulation writer has found a way out by entirely ignoring Matthew 24:37–39 as evidence of the time of the parousia.

There is, however, clear Scriptural proof to support the third of the above alternatives. 2 Thessalonians 2:8 does not refer to the parousia of the Lord but to the *manifestation* thereof. This manifestation is only one aspect of the parousia. The two words "manifestation of" give an entirely different meaning to this passage than it would have if these words had been omitted, and as sometimes quoted in support of the post-tribulation view. In fact, the preposition *of* has even been replaced by the conjunction *and,* to make it read "by the manifestation and *parousia.*" This violates the text in the original.

It must also be observed that the lawless one shall not be destroyed by the manifestation of the Lord, but by the manifestation of His parousia. It is His presence, subsequent to His arrival, that shall be manifested.

A manifestation is that which makes evident to

the senses, especially to the sight, something already in existence. It is the Lord's presence subsequent to an earlier arrival that is here said to be manifested. This presence must necessarily be veiled, or unseen from the time of the arrival until the time of its manifestation.

The word in the original here translated manifestation is said to mean "a shining forth." This is in accord with the use of the word *brightness* in the Authorized Version. The manifestation, then, shall be the sudden shining forth upon the lawless one of the great divine glory of the Lord's presence. By this shining forth the lawless one is brought to nought.

An illustration will be helpful. During a summer storm, the heavens are covered with clouds. The day becomes dark, almost as night, the lightning flashes, the thunder rolls. As the storm passes, with its destruction, almost unexpectedly the clouds break and the sun shines forth in all its glory. The sun is present during the storm, but its presence is veiled by the clouds. It becomes manifest when the clouds break.

The day of the Lord, which begins with the tribulation, as has been seen, shall be a day of clouds, a cloudy day. It shall be a day of darkness, even gross darkness. The description of the tribulation begins with the sound of thunder (Rev. 6:1). The lightning shall flash and destruction shall come upon the earth. The power of darkness under the leadership of the lawless one shall carry on its God-defying work. Then through the broken clouds the presence of the

Lord shall shine forth in a blaze of glory and the lawless one shall be brought to nought.

The intensity of that burst of glory can, in a small measure, be understood when it is remembered that Moses had to put a veil over his face to protect the people from the brightness with which it shone when he came out of the cloud from the presence of God even though he had not seen God's face.

There is, however, more evidence of the veiled presence of the Lord during the tribulation than that shown by the meaning of the word *manifestation*. The clouds that will be seen during the day of the Lord indicate His veiled presence during that time.

God's presence with the nation Israel from the time of the departure from Egypt was evidenced by a cloud, but He was never seen by them. It was a veiled presence. And it must be remembered that God is again dealing with Israel during the tribulation period. It shall be the seventieth week of Israel.

The following passages tell of God's veiled presence with Israel.

Of them, as they left Egypt, it is written: "And the LORD went before them by day in a pillar of a cloud, to lead them the way; and by night in a pillar of fire, to give them light" (Ex. 13:21).

When they were pursued by the Egyptians the pillar of the cloud stood between them and the Egyptians to whom "it was a cloud and darkness," but it gave light to the children of Israel (Ex. 14:20; cf. v. 24).

A thick cloud was the evidence that the Lord spoke to Moses. "And the LORD said unto Moses, Lo, I come unto thee in a thick cloud, that the people may hear when I speak with thee, and believe thee for ever" (Ex. 19:9).

When the Ten Commandments were delivered, the Lord came "down in the sight of all the people upon mount Sinai" (Ex. 19:11) and "there were thunders and lightnings, and a thick cloud upon the mount" (v. 16).

When Moses went up into the mount to receive the tables of stone a cloud covered the mount (Ex. 24:12, 15).

When the work on the tabernacle was finished, "Then a cloud covered the tent of the congregation" (Ex. 40:34).

"And when the cloud was taken up from over the tabernacle, the children of Israel went forward in all their journeys: but if the cloud were not taken up, then they journeyed not till the day that it was taken up." This was so "throughout all their journeys" (Ex. 40:36–38).

When the Lord came down to take of the spirit that was upon Moses and give it to the seventy elders, He came down in a cloud (Num. 11:25).

When Aaron and Miriam had spoken against Moses the Lord came down in the pillar of the cloud (Num. 12:1, 5, 9–10).

When Moses reviewed to the new generation of Israel the scene at Horeb (Sinai) he said, "And ye came near and stood under the mountain; and the mountain burned with fire unto the midst of heaven, with darkness, clouds, and thick darkness. And the LORD spake unto you out of the midst of the fire: ye heard the voice of the words, but saw no similitude" (Deut. 4:11–12). The Lord's presence was veiled by the clouds.

When the ark of the covenant of the Lord was brought into the temple built by Solomon, "the cloud filled the house of the LORD, . . . the glory of the LORD filled the house of the LORD" (1 Kings 8:10–11).

Every mention of the cloud or clouds in the history of Israel, from the time of their departure from Egypt, denotes a veiled presence of the Lord in His dealings with them.

When God caused the history of the seventieth week of Israel to be written in advance, He did not fail to show that then also the cloud would be present.

The word of the Lord through Ezekiel declared: "For the day is near, even the day of the LORD is near, a cloudy day" (30:3).

In Joel 2:3 the day of the Lord is declared to be a "day of darkness and of gloominess, a day of clouds and thick darkness." In Zephaniah 1:15 it is described as "a day of . . . darkness and gloominess, a day of clouds and thick darkness." These statements are almost identical with the words of Moses describing the scene at Horeb, "darkness, clouds, and thick darkness."

Surely the faithful remnant, the 144,000 servants

of God, of the twelve tribes of Israel, shall be conversant with the Old Testament. On seeing the cloudy heaven they will recognize the presence of the Lord in those clouds. To them the clouds will be what the cloudy pillar and the cloud upon the tabernacle were to their forefathers in the wilderness. No other evidence of the Lord's presence with His faithful remnant during those days is to be found in the Bible. Consistency demands that the clouds of Israel's seventieth week shall be given the same meaning as those of the rest of their national life.

A cloud is also related to the Lord's presence to judge a Gentile nation. "Behold the LORD rideth upon a swift cloud, and shall come into Egypt: and the idols of Egypt shall be moved at his presence, and the heart of Egypt shall melt in the midst of it" (Isa. 19:1).

The coming of the Son of man as in the days of Noah, to bring destruction upon an unsuspecting world, is the arrival aspect of the parousia. The clouds during the day of the Lord are the evidence of His subsequent presence. The shining forth of the parousia by which the lawless one is brought to nought is the manifestation of His presence.

This sheds much light upon the true meaning of the parousia and simplifies the interpretation of events related thereto.

In the light of the above it is not difficult to see a veiled presence of the Son of man, meting out judgment upon the ungodly world. As the pillar of the cloud was a light to Israel as they crossed the Red Sea, and darkness to the Egyptians, so the clouds of the day of the Lord shall be to the faithful of Israel a sign of the veiled presence of the Son of man, but darkness, yes, gross darkness, to the world. As the Lord looked unto the hosts of the Egyptians through the pillar of fire and of the cloud, and troubled them (Ex. 14:24), so shall the Son of man look through the clouds and trouble the world during the tribulation.

When the manifestation of the Lord's parousia shall destroy the lawless one, "Then shall appear the sign of the Son of man in heaven: and then shall all the tribes of the earth mourn, and they shall see the Son of man coming in the clouds of heaven with power and great glory" (Matt. 24:30). The emphasis here is upon the fact that the tribes of the earth shall *see* Him rather than on His coming. This is borne out by the statement: "Then shall appear the sign of the Son of man." Then He will be recognized. The words of Zechariah also support this thought: "And they shall look upon me whom they have pierced" (12:10). It is the *sight* of Him, the manifestation of Him, that will cause all the tribes of the earth to mourn.

This coming is not called the parousia. It is not said that He descends from heaven, or comes out of His place as in Isaiah 26:21. It will be a coming to earth in the clouds by which He has been veiled during the tribulation period. In these passages is seen a manifestation of the Son of man to all the tribes of the earth, including Israel. This will be after the tribulation.

The Church, God's heavenly people, does not belong to the tribes of the earth. Nor is she mentioned as witnessing the coming of the Son of man in the clouds. The glorious appearing of the great God and Saviour Jesus Christ (Titus 2:13) to the Church must be an entirely different event. The time of the appearing to the Church is not directly revealed. Because it will be accompanied by another event it is possible to ascertain the time thereof. John wrote: "Beloved, . . . it doth not yet appear what we shall be: but we know that, when he shall appear, we shall be like him; for we shall see him as he is" (1 John 3:2).

It is therefore at His appearing that all believers will be transformed into His likeness. According to 1 Corinthians 15:52 this transformation will occur "in a moment, in the twinkling of an eye" at the same time that the dead shall be raised incorruptible. When the dead in Christ shall rise, "then we which are alive and remain shall be caught up together with them in the clouds, to meet the Lord in the air" (1 Thess. 4:17). The glorious appearing of the Lord Jesus Christ to the Church, then, must be at the exact time of the rapture. This has already been shown to be before the tribulation. As the manifestation of the Son of man to all the tribes of the earth, including Israel, shall be after the tribulation these must be two separate events.

Having established the Lord's coming before the tribulation and His presence during that time, it is not difficult to accept the possibility of more than one appearing or manifestation during that time. The spiritual body, the Church, made up of all who are His own, is ready to see Him when He comes. Not so the sinful world, nor even Israel. The purging work of the tribulation must be accomplished before the tribes of the earth can behold Him. A similar condition prevailed at the end of the Lord's first advent to earth. During the days of His earthly ministry He was seen by both those who received Him and those who rejected Him. After His resurrection, He showed Himself only to believers. "God . . . shewed him openly; not to all the people, but unto witnesses chosen before of God" (Acts 10:40–41).

It should not seem strange then that at His second advent He should first show Himself to His Church, His body, before He shows Himself to Israel and the tribes of the earth.

It has been widely held by pre-tribulationists that there will be two separate comings, one before the tribulation, at which the Church will be raptured, and one after that time when Christ shall come to the earth in the clouds of heaven with power and great glory.

Because the manifestation by which the wicked is brought to nought is definitely one aspect of the parousia, it would seem that so also is the coming in the clouds of heaven. Whether this is an event during the subsequent presence of the parousia or a separate coming is not vital to this discussion. This is also true of other references to a coming after the tribulation. The word *parousia* establishes a pre-tribulation coming at which the Church shall be raptured, and that is the essential point at issue.

CHAPTER 10

Not Appointed unto Wrath

1 Thessalonians 4:16–17 and 5:1–11

F OR the Lord himself shall descend from heaven
with a shout, with the voice of the archangel, and
with the trump of God: and the dead in Christ shall
rise first: then we which are alive and remain shall
be caught up together with them in the clouds, to
meet the Lord in the air: and so shall we ever be
with the Lord" (vs. 16–17).

"But of the times and seasons, brethren, ye have
no need that I write unto you. For yourselves know
perfectly that the day of the Lord so cometh as a
thief in the night. For when they shall say, Peace and
safety; then sudden destruction cometh upon them,
as travail upon a woman with child; and they shall
not escape" (vs. 1–3).

"But ye, brethren, are not in darkness, that that
day should overtake you as a thief. Ye are all the
children of light, and the children of the day: we are
not of the night, nor of darkness" (vs. 4–5).

"Therefore let us not sleep, as do others; but let
us watch and be sober. For they that sleep sleep in
the night; and they that be drunken are drunken in
the night. But let us, who are of the day, be sober,
putting on the breastplate of faith and love; and for
an helmet, the hope of salvation" (vs. 6–8).

"For God hath not appointed us to wrath, but to obtain salvation by our Lord Jesus Christ, who died for us, that, whether we wake or sleep, we should live together with him. Wherefore comfort yourselves together" (vs. 9–11).

As the separation into chapters four and five breaks the continuity, the passage is quoted without the chapter division.

This passage has had partial consideration in the chapter on the parousia. There it was seen that the Lord shall descend from heaven not only to rapture the Church but also to bring in the day of trouble for Israel and the dark days of destruction and the vengeance and wrath of God upon the unsuspecting dwellers of the earth. Because this coming must precede the tribulation so must also the rapture. But there is much more here to show that the Church shall not pass through the tribulation.

In verses 16 and 17 Paul told of the coming of the Lord to raise the dead in Christ and to rapture the Church. In so doing, he used the first person "we."

In verses 1 to 3 he wrote about an entirely different matter. The day of the Lord shall come unexpectedly as a thief in the night with sudden destruction from which there will be no escape. These verses are introduced by the conjunction of contrast, *but,* and in referring to those upon whom the destruction shall come he used the third person, *them* and *they.*

Because of this language it is clear that there will be two groups, each exclusive of the other; the one shall be raptured, the other shall be struck by destruction. The fact that Paul first told the Thessalonian believers that they will be raptured, before he wrote about the destruction of the day of the Lord, must have assured them of full deliverance from that day. It should also so assure everyone who believes in Christ today.

Paul gave additional assurance that the "brethren" shall have no part in that day of darkness, even thick darkness. "But ye, brethren, are not in darkness, that that day should overtake you as a thief." All believers have been delivered from the power of darkness and translated into the kingdom of God's dear Son (Col. 1:13). They have been called out of darkness into the marvelous light of God (1 Peter 2:9). "For ye were sometimes darkness, but now are ye light in the Lord" (Eph. 5:8).

Because of this position of every believer, Paul completely excludes the possibility of the day of the Lord, which is a day of gross darkness for those who are darkness, coming upon believers. Before being delivered from the power of darkness that possibility existed, but not after being called into the marvelous light of God. Because the thief comes at night, it is impossible for him to overtake those who are of the day. Likewise the day of the Lord, which is a day of darkness, cannot overtake the children of light.

Jesus said: "I am the light of the world: he that followeth me shall not walk in darkness, but shall have the light of life" (John 8:12). That day of thick darkness is for those who have refused to come to

Him who is the light of the world. Those that follow Him shall not "walk" through that day of *gross* darkness.

Some say that the expression, "overtake you as a thief," merely means that the day of the Lord shall not come unexpectedly upon believers. This position is untenable in view of the meaning of the words: "cometh as a thief." The difference between a thief and a robber is the thief always comes secretly while a robber comes openly. If a thief cannot come secretly he cannot come at all. That is why thieves come during the night. Believers "are all children of the light, and children of the day." They "are not of the night, nor of darkness." This eliminates the possibility of secrecy and thereby prevents the thief from coming.

But there is even a greater reason why the day of the Lord cannot come as a thief. Another has come who prevents the thief from doing his work. Jesus said: "The thief cometh not, but for to steal, and to kill, and to destroy: I am come that they may have life, and that they might have it more abundantly" (John 10:10). When He came the first time, He came to do the very opposite of that which the thief comes to do.

When the day of the Lord shall come as a thief in the night upon all who are in darkness, to kill and destroy, then He who came to give life shall come again to deliver all who have received life from Him from that destruction. Then shall they, to the fullest, experience the more abundant life, a life of eternal fellowship with Him. That day to the Church will be a complete deliverance from all that the thief represents.

There is an even stronger assurance that the Church will be raptured before the wrath of the day of the Lord comes. "For God hath not appointed you unto wrath." What wrath? This must refer in particular to the wrath of the time mentioned in the immediate context, the day of the Lord. It must be the wrath that God shall pour on the vessels of wrath fitted for destruction, after He has made known the riches of His glory upon the Church.

The wrath of God is seen as accompanying spiritual darkness, and as coming upon the children of disobedience. "For the wrath of God is revealed from heaven against all ungodliness and unrighteousness of men, who hold the truth in unrighteousness" (Rom. 1:18). "But after thy hardness and impenitent heart treasurest up unto thyself wrath against the day of wrath and revelation of the righteous judgment of God" (Rom. 2:5).

Not once is it said that wrath will come upon the children of light. On the contrary, there is assurance of deliverance from wrath. "Much more then, being now justified by his blood, we shall be saved from [the] wrath through him" (Rom. 5:9). "To wait for his Son from heaven, . . . even Jesus, which delivered us from the wrath to come" (1 Thess. 1:10).

The message of the one "like unto the Son of man" (Rev. 1:13) given to the Church in Philadelphia confirms the revelation given through Paul and reassures believers that they will not pass through the tribulation. "Because thou hast kept the word of my patience, I also will keep thee from the hour of temptation, which shall come upon all the world, to try them that dwell upon the earth" (Rev. 3:10). Immediately after these words follows a promise of His soon coming. "Behold, I come quickly." Once more His coming is promised in connection with deliverance from the tribulation.

All these passages bring a comforting assurance that the Church shall not pass through the tribulation with its wrath.

Again Paul used the important word *but*. "But to obtain salvation by our Lord Jesus Christ." This salvation is in contrast to the wrath that shall come upon the children of darkness during the day of the Lord. It must be, therefore, deliverance from that wrath. There is no middle ground. It shall be wrath for those upon whom the day of the Lord comes. It shall be salvation from wrath for the Church.

This salvation shall be by Jesus Christ "Who died for us." Thus, His death is set forth as the guarantee of deliverance from wrath and that which will be accomplished by this salvation is that "we [the Church] should live together with Him."

In this passage from 1 Thessalonians, then, Paul wrote about two distinct groups as indicated by the use of "we," "the children of light" and "they," "the children of darkness." When the Lord shall descend from heaven the children of light shall be caught up to meet the Lord in the air to be forever with Him.

This salvation shall be by Jesus Christ who died for them. Upon the children of darkness shall come sudden destruction, even the wrath of the day of the Lord.

To hold that the Church shall pass through the tribulation is to deny the clear-cut separation of these two positions. It also destroys the comfort that comes from the words, "God hath not appointed us unto wrath, but . . . salvation," with which Paul said they should comfort themselves together.

Verses 6 to 8 have been left until now so as not to break the continuity of the explanation. In these verses some see a warning to believers to watch and be sober lest the day of the Lord should come upon them as a thief. To warn is to give notice of possible approaching danger or evil. The possibility of a child of light being overtaken by the day of wrath is not even intimated. Therefore, this cannot be construed as a warning. To so construe these verses is to imply that a child of light can become a child of the night and of darkness by not being sober and watching. This adds works to grace and denies the basic principle of grace that on the sole merits of Jesus Christ, every believer has a perfect and unalterable standing before God.

That which is here said is an admonition to watch and be sober. It is to look for the blessed hope, the glorious appearing of the great God and Saviour Jesus Christ. It is to wait for God's Son from heaven. It is to love His appearing. To be sober means to keep from being absorbed by the things of the world.

This admonition is based on the certainty of the position as children of light, and not of darkness.

Under grace, God always reminds the believer of a sure and unalterable provision which He has made, apart from any human effort, and then asks the believer to live a life in harmony therewith.* This admonition is in perfect accord with that method. Even in this admonition is seen added proof of the certainty of deliverance from the tribulation, the day of the Lamb's wrath.

In view of these clear, direct, and positive statements, one thing is certain, those who are "in Christ" shall not pass through that period in which the wrath of God is poured forth upon the earth. If the rapture is to take place after the tribulation then it rests upon those who so hold to explain how the Church can remain on earth during that period and still be delivered from its wrath. The Bible offers no other explanation than the pre-tribulation rapture.

* A more complete explanation of God's method under grace is given in the writer's book, *Disciplined by Grace*.

CHAPTER 11

The Restrainer Taken Out of the Way

Now we beseech you, brethren, touching the coming of our Lord Jesus Christ, and our gathering together unto him; 2 to the end that ye be not quickly shaken from your mind, nor yet be troubled, either by spirit, or by word, or by epistle as from us, as that the day of the Lord is just at hand; 3 let no man beguile you in any wise: for it will not be, except the falling away come first, and the man of sin be revealed, the son of perdition, 4 he that opposeth and exalteth himself against all that is called God or that is worshipped; so that he sitteth in the temple of God, setting himself forth as God. 5 Remember ye not, that, when I was yet with you, I told you these things? 6 And now ye know that which restraineth, to the end that he may be revealed in his own season. 7 For the mystery of lawlessness doth already work: only there is one that restraineth now, until he be taken out of the way. 8 And then shall be revealed the lawless one, whom the Lord Jesus shall slay with the breath of his mouth, and bring to nought by the manifestation of his coming; 9 even he, whose coming is according to the working of Satan with all power and signs and lying wonders, 10 and with all deceit of unrighteousness for them that perish; because they received not the love of the truth, that they might be saved. 11 And for this cause God send-eth them a working of error, that they should believe a lie: 12 that they all might be judged who believed not the truth, but had pleasure in un-righteousness.

"13 But we are bound to give thanks to God always for you, brethren beloved of the Lord, for that God chose you from the beginning unto salvation in sanctification of the Spirit and belief of the truth: 14 whereunto he called you through our gospel, to the obtaining of the glory of our Lord Jesus Christ. 15 So then, brethren, stand fast, and hold the traditions which ye were taught, whether by word, or by epistle of ours.

"16 Now our Lord Jesus Christ himself, and God our Father who loved us and gave us eternal comfort and good hope through grace, 17 comfort your hearts and establish them in every good work and word."

The foregoing Chapter 2 of Second Thessalonians has been copied in full from the American Standard (Revised) Version which eliminates an archaic word, the meaning of which has been completely changed since the Authorized Version was made. It also corrects the mistranslation, "the day of Christ," into "the day of the Lord." This mistranslation in the Authorized Version has caused much confusion. Paul here wrote about the same day as in 1 Thessalonians 5, the day of the Lord's wrath and vengeance. To recognize this is important in the interpretation of the chapter. In this chapter Paul unmistakably wrote touching the coming (parousia) of the

Lord Jesus Christ and the rapture. According to a note in the American Standard (Revised) Version he wrote "in behalf of" that event.

The Thessalonians were concerned that the day of the Lord was at hand, or present, as some translate this passage. Paul had assured them in his first letter that they should have no part in that day but would be caught up to be with the Lord when that day shall come upon those on earth. In the passage under consideration, Paul assured them that the day of the Lord was not at hand because certain things must precede that day. A falling-away must first come and the man of sin must be revealed. This man of sin, the lawless one, will exalt himself against all that is called God and will sit in the temple of God and be worshipped as God. But the coming of that lawless one will be restrained by some influence. Some Person will also restrain until that Person is taken out of the way. After that shall the lawless one be revealed. In short, before the day of the Lord comes the lawless one must be revealed, but he cannot be revealed until One who restrains the working of lawlessness is taken out of the way. Here in simple language is the order of events before the day of the Lord can come.

But what does this have to do with the rapture of the Church? Just this, the One who restrains the working of lawlessness is inseparably identified with the Church.

In order to understand who it is that restrains, it is necessary to have a full view of the lawless one. In addition to being the lawless one, he is the man of sin, the son of perdition, the Wicked. He "opposeth and exalteth himself against all that is called God or that is worshipped; so that he sitteth in the temple of God, setting himself forth as God." His "coming is according to the working of Satan with all power and signs and lying wonders." He must be the arch-representative of the powers of darkness.

In the restraint of him is seen a great spiritual contest. Because the workings of the wicked one are spiritual, the One who restrains him must also be a spiritual Being. He must be stronger than Satan who energizes the wicked one. Of the Restrainer Paul wrote, "there is one that restraineth now, until he [a person] be taken out of the way." Paul wrote *now* nineteen hundred years ago and the Restrainer still restrains. Only a divine being can be said to be spiritual, stronger than Satan, and have exercised a restraining influence for more than nineteen hundred years. He that restrains must, yes *must,* be One of the triune Godhead.

As the Holy Spirit is the only member of the Godhead that has been residentially active on earth during these nineteen hundred years He must be the One who restrains and will continue to restrain until He be taken out of the way. Shortly before Jesus left this earth He promised to send the Comforter, i.e., the Holy Spirit, to the earth (John 16:7).

God's Word clearly teaches that the Holy Spirit is the One who counteracts the influence of Satan during the Church age. It is said that "the God of this world [Satan] hath blinded the minds of them which believe not" (2 Cor. 4:4). The Holy Spirit reproves the world of sin, of righteousness, and of judgment (John 16:8). Through this convicting work of the Spirit, men and women are taken out of darkness and brought into the Church.

The Holy Spirit works in and through the Church of Christ. He guides the Church into all truth (John 16:13). He empowers the Church to witness (Acts 1:8). It is through Him that victory is won over spiritual darkness and wickedness. Paul wrote: "For we wrestle not against flesh and blood, but against principalities, against powers, against the rulers of the darkness of this world, against spiritual wickedness in high places." The offensive weapons of this warfare against Satan's rule are "the sword of the Spirit, which is the word of God," and "praying always with all prayer and supplication in the Spirit" (Eph. 6:12, 17–18).

John wrote: "Ye are of God, little children, and have overcome them [i.e., those who have the spirit of antichrist, which shall come]; because greater is he [the Holy Spirit] that is in you, than he [Satan] that is in the world" (1 John 4:4). Notice, it is in overcoming the spirit of antichrist that believers are encouraged by the fact that the Holy Spirit is greater than Satan. The coming of the lawless one is the culmination of the spirit of antichrist. This passage clearly teaches that the spirit of antichrist, which is by Satan, is overcome by the Holy Spirit in the children of God.

The taking out of the way of the Holy Spirit be-

fore the lawless one, the man of sin, can be revealed
and followed by sudden destruction falling upon the
dwellers of the earth is not without precedent. In the
days of Noah, God said: "My Spirit shall not always
strive with man" (Gen. 6:3). He then gave mankind
one hundred and twenty years. After that the flood
came and carried them all away. While all the details are not the same, in both cases, the work of the
Holy Spirit to restrain sin is brought to an end. Instead of pleading with man, God sent destruction.
The fact that Jesus likened the days of Noah and the
destruction by the flood to the days of His parousia
and the destruction that shall then come, adds weight
to the comparison of the restraint by the Holy Spirit
before both events occur.

It is evident, then, that He who restrains is the
Holy Spirit and that which restrains is the Church.
The Holy Spirit must be taken out of the way before the man of sin, the lawless one, can be revealed.
When He is taken out of the way He returns to
heaven, from whence He was sent by the Lord Jesus
Christ after He had ascended into heaven. Remember, the day of the Lord cannot come until the lawless one shall be revealed and he cannot be revealed
before the Holy Spirit returns to heaven. The Holy
Spirit, then, must return to heaven before the tribulation commences, because the lawless one exercises
His great power during that time.

This return of the Holy Spirit to heaven must not
be interpreted as a complete withdrawal from earth
because He, being One of the Godhead, is omnipres-

ent. It means a return in the sense that He came at the very beginning of the Church age as described in John 14:16; 16:7; Acts 1:8; 2:2. Just as He was present before that time, so shall He be present after He has been taken out of the way.

When the Holy Spirit leaves the earth and goes to heaven so must also the instrument through which He now works, even the Church. It cannot be otherwise. Before the Lord departed from this earth He promised: "I will pray the Father, and he shall give you another Comforter, that he may abide with you for ever; even the Spirit of truth" (John 14:16–17). Because the Spirit abides forever there can be no separation of the Holy Spirit from the believer. When He leaves the earth so must also the Church, and this is before the tribulation begins.

But there is more evidence. All believers are sealed with the Holy Spirit until the day of redemption (Eph. 1:13–14). If the redemption of the bodies of believers does not take place when the Holy Spirit departs then the seal is broken and God's guarantee of a final redemption is gone. Furthermore, the Holy Spirit is the earnest of the believer's inheritance. God will not withdraw from the Church His guarantee of an inheritance. Surely, when the Holy Spirit is taken out of the way the Church must be taken with Him.

Consider now what would be the condition of the Church during the tribulation if she were to be left on earth, and the Holy Spirit were to be taken away from her, for it is clear that the Holy Spirit will not be on earth during that time, as He is in the present age of grace, indwelling believers.

Then there would be no Comforter (John 14:16) during those awful days of torment. But this is contrary to God's promise: "I will never leave thee, nor forsake thee." There would be none to show the believer the things of Christ (John 16:14). There would be none to teach all things (John 14:26) during those bewildering years. There would be a Church without power to resist Satan during the time that He is cast out from heaven upon the earth. There would be an impotent Church, a comfortless Church, an unguided Church during the most terrible days of the entire human history.

But this shall not be the fate of the Church because Paul was writing as "touching the coming of our Lord Jesus Christ, and our gathering together unto him" (2 Thess. 2:1) and that which he said about the Holy Spirit being taken out of the way is directly related to that glorious prospect of the Church.

Inasmuch as Jesus had said that the Holy Spirit could not be sent unless He departed, it must be of real importance that Paul related the departure of the Holy Spirit from the earth with the coming again of the Lord to receive His own unto Himself. Before the Holy Spirit was sent Jesus comforted, guided, and empowered His followers. When He went, that work was given to the Holy Spirit and in addition thereto the ministry of glorifying Christ to the believer. When Christ comes to receive His own unto Himself, into the many mansions that He has prepared for them, the Holy Spirit will not need to glorify Him for they shall see Him as He is. They will behold Him in all His glory and will share that glory with Him. The glory of Jesus Christ that is now being shown the Church by the Holy Spirit, and which she shall behold face to face shall surely not be dimmed by a period of tribulation which Jesus described as so terrible that none has ever been like it nor ever shall be thereafter. The infinite grace of God will not permit that to happen to the objects of His grace.

When He who restrains is taken out of the way, the man of sin, the lawless one shall be revealed and, being empowered by Satan, shall work lying wonders with all deceit and unrighteousness for them that perish. Because these have not received the truth and been saved, God will send upon them a working of error so that they will believe a lie. Then judgment will come upon them because they have not believed the truth but have had pleasure in unrighteousness. This judgment must be that which comes during the day of the Lord because that is the time which cannot come until He that restrains is taken out of the way.

Notice carefully that this judgment is upon those that believe not the truth. It is for those who reject Him who came full of grace and truth, He who is the truth.

Here again, as in Chapter 5 of First Thessalonians, is found that little but most important word of contrast. "But we are bound to give thanks to God always for you, brethren beloved of the Lord, for that God chose you from the beginning unto salvation in sanctification of the Spirit and belief of the truth . . . to the obtaining of the glory of our Lord Jesus Christ." The brethren are in contrast to those that believe not the truth. But the contrast is even more important. Those who believe not the truth shall perish being judged in the day of the Lord. Those who believe are chosen unto salvation and "to the obtaining of the glory of our Lord Jesus Christ." This must be the manifestation of that glory which Jesus told His Father that He had given to them that believe on Him (John 17:22). And when shall this glory be obtained? It cannot be as long as believers are in the present corruptible and mortal bodies. It must be when they shall see Him as He is and become like Him (1 John 3:2). It can only be when they will be with Him and behold His glory which the Father has given Him (John 17:24). And where shall that be? Again, it must be in the many mansions of the Father's house which He went to prepare.

If these words mean anything, they mean that the Church shall be saved from the judgments of the tribulation. While the wicked world is experiencing the wrath of God, she shall be in glory with her Head and Lord.

The chapter closes with an assurance of the love

of the Lord Jesus Christ and eternal comfort and good hope through grace that the hearts may be established in every good work and word. Truly the hope of glory instead of tribulation does establish unto every good work and word.

CHAPTER 12

At the Last Trump

BEHOLD, I shew you a mystery; We shall not all sleep, but we shall all be changed, in a moment, in the twinkling of an eye, at the last trump: for the trumpet shall sound, and the dead shall be raised incorruptible, and we shall be changed" (1 Cor. 15:51–52). That this event is the resurrection of the dead in Christ and the rapture of the Church cannot be questioned. The important question is, What is "the last trump" and when shall it be sounded? Various interpretations have been suggested, mostly without Scriptural corroboration. The following seems to harmonize more nearly with the teaching of the Scriptures than others that have been presented.

The Bible says much about the blowing of trumpets. There were trumpets blown by men, by the priests of the Levitical priesthood, and by warriors. Trumpets are also blown by angels, but the greatest of all is the blowing of God's own trumpet. The first question then is, On what plane is the last trump? Is it a trumpet blown by man, by an angel, or is it God's trumpet? Surely the greatness of the event suggests the last.

The answer to this question is easily found. Paul, in 1 Thessalonians 4:16–17, taught that at the coming (parousia) of the Lord "the Lord himself shall descend from heaven . . . with the trump of God: and the dead in Christ shall rise first: then we which are alive and remain shall be caught up together with them in the clouds, to meet the Lord in the air." This must be the same trump as "the last trump" of 1 Corinthians 15:52 because in both verses the dead believers are said to rise when it is sounded.

From the above it is certain that "the last trump" is the trump of God and that the Lord Himself descends from heaven with it. In the search for "the last trump" one must, then, be guided by the fact that it is God's own trumpet, sounded by the Lord Himself. In view of this one would hardly be willing to contend that the last trumpet of God is the last of a series of trumpets blown by the priests of the Aaronic priesthood. These were not in a class with the trumpet of God. Remembering that the angels are only a little higher than man, it is just as contrary to the laws of logic to say that "the last trump," which is God's own trumpet, is the last of a series of trumpets blown by angels. Both men and angels are creatures of God. They cannot sound the trumpet of the Creator. No, the Lord Himself shall descend from heaven with the trump of God. This limits the inquiry to a study of trumpets sounded by God.

In former years, every morning one would hear the school bells ringing. The first bell rang at eight-thirty o'clock, the second bell at fifteen minutes to nine and the last bell at five minutes to nine. All three of these bells called the children to school, but the second bell was a more urgent call than the first, and the last bell was very urgent. This was repeated five days each week so there was a last bell each day, in fact twice each day, because the three bells were repeated in the afternoons. The last bell was the last of the series of three all of the same kind.

At nine o'clock each morning another bell was rung; it was the tardy bell. It was never called the last bell because it had a different meaning than the other three.

So also "the last trump" is the last of a series of at least two trumpets of the same kind and for the same purpose. As "the last trump" shall be the trump of God there must be a first trumpet which is ascribed to God. That trumpet is not hard to find.

The first trumpet mentioned in the Bible is that sounded at the giving of the law from Mount Sinai. The blowing of this trumpet, its purpose, and the manifestations accompanying it are given in detail in Exodus nineteen. "The LORD said unto Moses, Lo, I come unto thee in a thick cloud, that the people may hear when I speak with thee, and believe thee for ever. . . . Go unto the people, and sanctify them to day and to morrow, and let them wash their clothes, and be ready against the third day: for the third day the LORD will come down in the sight of all the people upon Mount Sinai" (vs. 9–11). "When the trumpet soundeth long, they shall come up to the mount" (v. 13).

"And it came to pass on the third day in the morning, that there were thunders and lightnings, and a thick cloud upon the mount, and the voice of the trumpet exceeding loud; so that all the people that was in the camp trembled. And Moses brought forth the people out of the camp to meet God; and they stood at the nether part of the mount. And mount Sinai was altogether on a smoke, because the LORD descended upon it in fire: and the smoke ascended as the smoke of a furnace, and the whole mount quaked greatly, and when the voice of the trumpet sounded long, and waxed louder and louder, Moses spake, and God answered him by a voice. And the LORD came down upon mount Sinai, on the top of the mount" (vs. 16–20).

The things to be observed here are: (1) God descended (from heaven) upon Mount Sinai. (2) The sounding of the trumpet was the signal for the people to come up to the Mount. (3) This was in the morning at the very beginning of the day when the law was to be given. (4) The trumpet was accompanied by thunders and lightnings and a thick cloud. Smoke ascended as the smoke of a furnace and the whole Mount quaked. (5) The people met God personally as man had never before met Him since sin entered the human race. (6) The people trembled at the voice of the trumpet.

This first trumpet spoken of in the Bible is unquestionably a trumpet of God. In that it grew louder and louder it is seen to be supernatural. It displayed the terror of God and produced fear and trembling in the hearts of the people. It is the first trump of God.

The writer of the letter to the Hebrews also described this event. His purpose in so doing was to contrast it with the glorious position of the believer. "For ye are not come unto the mount that might be touched, and that burned with fire, nor unto blackness, and darkness, and tempest, and the sound of a trumpet and the voice of words; which voice they that heard intreated that the word should not be spoken to them any more: (for they could not endure that which was commanded . . . and so terrible was the sight, that Moses said, I exceedingly fear and quake:)" (Heb. 12:18–21).

That which occurred that day at Mount Sinai was at the very beginning of the age of the law, which is called the ministration of death and the ministration of condemnation (2 Cor. 3:7, 9).

Israel nationally is still under the curse of the Mosaic law which they failed to fulfill. When, in the seventieth week of Israel, God again turns to them they shall pass through the day of Jacob's trouble not only because they have failed to keep the law, but also because they rejected and crucified Him who came to take away the curse of the law.

Malachi, in his prophecy of the day of the Lord, added these significant words from the Lord: "Remember ye the law of Moses my servant, which I commanded unto him in Horeb for all Israel, with the statutes and judgments" (Mal. 4:4). That day will witness an outpouring of judgments upon Israel as never before. Judgments shall also come upon the Gentile nations.

It is, therefore, not unexpected to find that the day of the Lord will be ushered in by the sounding of a trumpet. "All ye inhabitants of the world, and dwellers on the earth, see ye, when he [the Lord] lifteth up an ensign on the mountains; and when he bloweth a trumpet, hear ye" (Isa. 18:3). This is the Lord's own call to the dwellers on the earth of impending judgment prior to the final regathering of Israel unto their land. "For afore the harvest, when the bud is perfect, and the sour grape is ripening in the flower, he shall both cut off the sprigs with pruning hooks, and take away and cut down the branches" (v. 5).

Zephaniah also told of a trumpet at the great day of the Lord. He calls it *the* trumpet which singles it out from among all others. He also describes the manifestations of God's fierce anger and terror that shall accompany the trumpet. Notice how similar they are to those of the first trumpet, that of Sinai. "The great day of the LORD is near, it is near, and hasteth greatly, even the voice of the day of the LORD: the mighty man shall cry there bitterly. That day is a day of wrath, a day of trouble and distress, a day of wasteness and desolation, a day of darkness and gloominess, a day of clouds and thick darkness, a day of the trumpet and alarm against fenced cities, and against high towers. And I will bring distress upon men, that they shall walk like blind men, because they have sinned against the LORD: and their blood shall be poured out as dust, and their flesh as the dung" (Zeph. 1:14–17).

Another important thing to consider is that at the beginning of the day of the Lord, He comes forth from heaven. Isaiah wrote, "Behold, the LORD cometh out of his place to punish the inhabitants of the earth for their iniquity" (26:21). This coming shall be *before* the judgments begin, in perfect agreement with the parousia of the Son of man.

Just as He descended on Sinai to sound the first trumpet so shall He come forth from heaven to sound the trumpet of the day of the Lord. This special trumpet of the day of the Lord not only has the same accompanying demonstrations as had the trumpet of Sinai but it shall also instill fear and trembling in the hearts of men. This is the second time the trumpet of God is sounded.

That this trumpet is sounded to usher in the day of the Lord seems certain because the trumpet was always used to call people together for convocation or battle, to sound alarm of impending danger, and to usher in great events and important periods of time. It is the trump to which Paul related the coming, yes, the very beginning of the day of the Lord (1 Thess. 4:15–16; 5:2–3).

One will search Scripture in vain to find that this trumpet of the fierce anger and terror of God is ever sounded again. It therefore becomes the last trumpet as well as the second. It is the only such trumpet mentioned in the Bible that can be called "the last trump" of God.

It is of special interest and importance to notice that at the first trumpet God descended from heaven in a thick cloud. At the second trumpet, the last trump, He also goes forth from heaven and then, too, is seen a thick cloud. When at Sinai the Lord came down in "the sight of all the people," Israel saw Him only in the terror-instilling manifestations that accompanied His coming because He was covered by a thick cloud. When He comes with the last trump the dwellers of the earth shall see Him only in His manifestations of wrath and fierce anger. But the Church shall see Him as He is in His glorious appearing, for "we know that, when he shall appear, we shall be like him; for we shall see him as he is" (1 John 3:2).

Because the beginning of the day of the Lord is the beginning of the tribulation, the last trump must, then, also come before that time. Furthermore, according to 1 Thessalonians 4:16, it will be at the parousia that the Lord shall descend with the trump of God. This also is evidence that the last trump will come before the tribulation because the parousia, according to Matthew 24:37–39, will be before any judgments fall upon an unsuspecting mankind.

Inasmuch as the believer does not "come unto the mount that might be touched, and that burned with fire, nor unto blackness, and darkness, and tempest" which was heralded by the first trumpet of God, he may be sure that he shall not come to the day of the Lord with its far greater manifestations of fire and darkness and tempest and gloom and wrath and fierce anger of God during which the judgments of the law shall be meted out and which shall be heralded by "the last trump." He is not under law, but under grace (Rom. 6:14).

Just as the parousia will mean grace to the Church and judgment to the dwellers of the earth, so the last trump will mean resurrection and glory for the Church and sudden destruction of the enemies of the Lord.

CHAPTER 13

The Argument from Silence

IN READING the record of the tribulation, beginning at the sixth chapter of Revelation and closing with the nineteenth, one cannot fail to be im-
pressed with the fact that there is no mention made
of the Church being on earth during that time. The
record is not only silent about the presence of the
Church on earth, it is also silent concerning any
cause, or reason, why the Church should then be on
earth. There is complete silence respecting any purpose to be fulfilled thereby. There is also silence regarding any protection for the Church against the
torment of those years. This silence, while not in
itself a conclusive argument for the pre-tribulation
rapture of the Church, adds great weight to the direct arguments already presented. When, however,
the Bible supplies irrefutable reasons for this silence,
then this silence does become important evidence in
favor of the view that the Church will not be on
earth during that time.

Some think that they find mention of the Church
on earth during the tribulation in the use of the
word *saint* in 13:7. It is true that the members of the
Church are saints. But it is equally true that God's
people of the Old Testament are saints. So also are
those of the large multitude saved during the tribu-

lation who will not be part of the Church, but servants in God's temple. The faithful remnant of Israel
that will pass through the tribulation also qualify as
saints. In the absence of evidence that these are
Church saints, it must be concluded that these saints
either belong to God's chosen people, Israel, or those
saved during the tribulation, both of which will be
on earth during that period.

The absence of the Church from the earth during
the tribulation is indicated by the statements that
it shall "try them that dwell upon the earth" (3:10),
and, "Woe, woe, woe, to the inhabiters of the earth"
(8:13), as well as other references to them "that dwell
upon the earth."

The phrases, *dwell upon the earth,* and also *inhabit the earth,* are intensive expressions that mean
more than merely being present on the earth. The
meaning is to settle down, to live there fixedly. It is
an earthly citizenship. When God created man He
commanded Adam and Eve to replenish the earth, to
subdue it, and have dominion over that which was
thereon. By virtue of this, man became an earth
dweller. In fact, he was created for that purpose.

But man sinned and God called Abram out from
among the heathen, gave him a land, and promised
to make of him a great nation. This nation, Israel,
still remained as dwellers upon earth. All the promises to them, throughout the Bible, are of blessings
on the earth and particularly in the land of Palestine.
God's purposes for them are all to be fulfilled on
the earth. They remain dwellers upon earth. Here,

then, are seen two groups of dwellers upon the earth: the Gentiles and Israel. This condition existed until the death and resurrection of Christ. After that a third group is seen, the Church of God. Paul recognized these three distinct groups as "the Jews, . . . the Gentiles, . . . and the church of God" (1 Cor. 10:32).

Members of the Church are not earth dwellers. Of them it is said: "For our conversation [citizenship, A.S.V.] is in heaven; from whence also we look for the Saviour, the Lord Jesus Christ" (Phil. 3:20). This is so because God "hath raised us up together, and made us sit together in heavenly places in Christ Jesus" (Eph. 2:6). Jesus said: "Ye are not of the world, but I have chosen you out of the world, therefore the world hateth you" (John 15:19).

The promises of blessing to the Church are not earthly blessings to be enjoyed in the land of Palestine. On the contrary, she is blessed "with all spiritual blessings in heavenly places in Christ" (Eph. 1:3).

That the heathen are included among those that dwell upon the earth is clearly seen by the statement of Obadiah (v. 15): "For the day of the LORD is near upon all heathen," and that by Isaiah: "The indignation of the LORD is upon all nations" (34:2). The sealing of the twelve thousand of each of the twelve tribes of Israel as well as the fact that the tribulation is the day of Jacob's trouble is proof that Israel shall be on earth during that time.

The repeated mention of the dwellers, or inhabiters, of the earth as being in the tribulation, and the absence of any mention of the Church, and the fact that the Church has a heavenly citizenship, strongly indicate that the Church shall not pass through that period.

There is complete silence respecting any reason why the tribulation should come upon the Church. On the other hand it is said to be "the hour of trial [temptation, A.V.], that hour which is to come upon the whole world, to try them that dwell upon the earth" (Rev. 3:10, A.S.V.). "The day of the LORD shall be upon every one that is proud" (Isa. 2:12). One who is proud has an exaggerated estimate of himself. He does not humble himself as a sinner before God. The day of the Lord comes to destroy the sinners out of the land, and to "punish the world for their evil, and the wicked for their iniquity; and . . . cause the arrogancy of the proud to cease" (Isa. 13:9, 11).

Jeremiah, speaking the word of the Lord to Israel, said: "I have wounded thee with the wound of an enemy, with the chastisement of a cruel one, for the multitude of thine iniquity; because thy sins were increased" (30:14). Another reason why Israel shall pass through the tribulation is told by Ezekiel: "And I [Lord GOD] will purge out from among you the rebels, and them that transgress against me" (20:38).

Paul, in the same letter to the Thessalonians in which he told them that they were not appointed unto wrath but unto obtaining salvation, wrote that the wrath is come upon the Jews to the uttermost because they killed the Lord Jesus and forbade speaking to the Gentiles that they might be saved (1 Thess. 2:14–16). Their request, that "His blood be on us, and on our children" (Matt. 27:25), shall be fulfilled as they go through the great tribulation.

Are there any such causes for the Church to pass through that time of wrath? The Word of God is absolutely silent in this matter. In fact, it must be because none of these things can be applied to any member of the Church. All who are in the Church have humbled themselves and confessed themselves sinners before God. Sins have been forgiven "according to the riches of his grace; wherein he hath abounded toward us in all wisdom and prudence" (Eph. 1:7–8). They are no longer rebels, but have been reconciled to God by the cross (Eph. 2:16). They have been perfected forever by the one offering of Christ by which they are sanctified (Heb. 10:10, 14). They have not killed, but accepted, Jesus as Saviour and Lord. Having been justified by His blood, much more they shall by Him be saved from the wrath that comes upon the heathen and upon Israel.

This shows that not only is there complete silence concerning any cause for which the Church should go through the tribulation, but it is clearly taught that the reasons why the dwellers upon the earth must go through that time do not apply to the Church.

But the tribulation has an additional purpose over and above the punishment of the heathen and the chastising of Israel. Neither of these groups comes to an end in the tribulation. For Israel it is a time of purification that she may bring offerings acceptable unto God. "And he [the Lord] shall sit as a refiner and purifier of silver: and he shall purify the sons of Levi, and purge them as gold and silver, that they may offer unto the LORD an offering in righteousness. Then shall the offering of Judah and Jerusalem be pleasant unto the LORD" (Mal. 3:3–4).

Then shall Israel be willing and fit to carry out the purpose for which Abraham was called out of his father's house, to be a blessing to all families of the earth. Then "the Gentiles shall come to thy [Zion's] light, and kings to the brightness of thy rising" (Isa. 60:3). "And in his [the servant of the Lord's] name shall the Gentiles trust" (Matt. 12:21).

But before that time, even during the tribulation, shall a remnant of Israel be God's witnesses upon earth. One hundred forty-four thousand servants of God, twelve thousand of each tribe of Israel, shall be sealed so they cannot be hurt during that time.

One searches the Scriptures in vain to find any ministry that is said to be exercised by the Church upon the earth at that time, or any purpose to be accomplished. When the long-suffering of God shall come to an end and He pours His wrath upon the vessels of wrath, then the preaching of the gospel of the grace of God committed to the Church shall have come to an end. Then the last member of the Church will have been taken out of the world. Then God's purpose for the Church on earth will have been fulfilled. Herein is sufficient reason for the absolute silence concerning any purpose to be fulfilled by the Church during that time.

To hold that the Church shall pass through the tribulation together with the dwellers upon the earth is entirely out of harmony with God's purposes for the Church. It is contrary to all that the Scriptures reveal concerning the place in God's program of the Jews, the Gentiles, and the Church of God.

Still another silence must be considered. Not one word is said about any protection provided by God for the Church against the horrors and torment of those days. This silence is of the greatest possible importance in view of the fact that such protection shall be provided for the faithful of Israel.

At the very beginning of the tribulation, before any hurt is permitted to come upon the earth and the sea, the servants of God will be sealed in their foreheads. These servants of God cannot be mistaken as belonging to the Church for they are expressly said to be twelve thousand of each of the twelve tribes of Israel (Rev. 7:3–8).

When the fifth trumpet shall be sounded, locusts, with the power of scorpions, shall come out of the pit. To them shall be given to torment "those men which have not the seal of God in their foreheads." This torment shall last five months, "and in those days shall men seek death, and shall not find it" (Rev. 9:1–6). God's servants of Israel shall be protected against this torment. No protection for the Church is mentioned for those five months of torment. Shall the members of the Church suffer that torment? Shall they seek death and not find it? What comforting assurance do those who hold that the Church shall pass through the tribulation have to give of God's care during that time? God offers none. The only escape promised in the Bible is the rapture before the day of wrath commences.

The two witnesses who shall prophesy a thousand two hundred and three score days shall be given a means to protect themselves: "And if any man will hurt them, fire proceedeth out of their mouth, and devoureth their enemies: and if any man will hurt them, he must in this manner be killed" (Rev. 11:5).

Isaiah prophesying to Israel wrote: "Come, my people, enter thou into thy chambers, and shut thy doors about thee: hide thyself as it were for a little moment, until the indignation be overpast. For, behold, the LORD cometh out of His place to punish the inhabitants of the earth for their iniquity" (26:20–21).

There is a definite promise of protection for Israel in the following verse: "And the woman [Israel] fled into the wilderness, where she hath a place prepared of God, that they should feed her there a thousand two hundred and three score days" (Rev. 12:6). According to verses 13 and 14 of the same chapter this flight shall be made when Satan, cast out of heaven, shall persecute Israel. This protection shall last three and a half years, or to the end of the tribulation.

Yes, for the faithful remnant of Israel are given repeated assurances of protection, but not one word is said about protection for the Church. There is absolute silence about any such provision. Certainly, if the Church is not to be received into the many mansions of the Father's house before the tribulation starts, some revelation would have been given regarding her safekeeping on earth during those awful days of torment.

A very illuminating illustration of God's provision for the faithful of Israel through the tribulation and the removal of the Church from the earth before the tribulation is found in Luke 17:26–30. Noah went into the ark before the flood came and "destroyed them all." He and his family were carried by the ark safely *through* the waters of judgment. On the other hand, the righteous man Lot (2 Pet. 2:8) was *delivered out of* the wicked city of Sodom, a type of the world, to a place of safety before the judgment came. In fact, one of the angels who came to destroy Sodom said to Lot that he could do nothing until he, Lot, had come to a place of safety (Gen. 19:22).

Because of all these important facts a strong responsibility rests upon those who hold that the Church shall pass through the tribulation to show how all of this can be harmonized with their view.

CHAPTER 14

The Church in Heaven During the Tribulation

BECAUSE no evidence whatsoever is found to show that the Church will be on earth during the tribulation, it is reasonable to conclude that she will be in heaven. It is not, however, necessary to depend upon this conclusion alone. Certain great events for the Church will take place in heaven during that time.

Paul wrote: "For we must all appear before the judgment seat of Christ; that every one may receive the things done in his body, according to that he hath done, whether it be good or bad" (2 Cor. 5:10). This judgment seat must be in heaven because the things to be judged are those that have been done in the present bodies. Things will continue to be done in the body up to the very twinkling of an eye when the bodies of believers are changed and caught up to be with the Lord. It is also evident that appearing before the judgment seat of Christ must be the first experience of the Church in heaven because it is to be a judgment by Christ of the believers' works while on earth. All that is not acceptable to Him shall be done away at once. All things that belong to the earthly life need to be judged in preparation for the heavenly state.

This judgment seat is called the *bema*. This is the

word used for the judgment seat before which athletes in the Olympic games appeared to receive their crowns.

In another place Paul wrote: "Now if any man build upon this foundation [Jesus Christ] gold, silver, precious stones, wood, hay, stubble; every man's work shall be made manifest: for the day shall declare it, because it shall be revealed by fire; and the fire shall try every man's work of what sort it is. If any man's work abide which he hath built thereupon, he shall receive a reward. If any man's work shall be burned, he shall suffer loss: but he himself shall be saved; yet so as by fire" (1 Cor. 3:12–15).

Surely this event must come before the Church shall appear with Him in glory (Col. 3:4). No wood, hay, and stubble shall be seen in the glorious appearing with Him.

A second event is seen in heaven during the tribulation period in which the Church will have a very important part. It is the marriage of the Lamb. "And I heard as it were the voice of a great multitude, and as the voice of many waters, and as the voice of mighty thunderings, saying, Alleluia: for the Lord God omnipotent reigneth. Let us be glad and rejoice, and give honour to him: for the marriage of the Lamb is come, and his wife hath made herself ready. And to her was granted that she should be arrayed in fine linen, clean and white: for the fine linen is the righteousness of saints. And he saith unto me, Write, Blessed are they which are called unto the marriage supper of the Lamb" (Rev. 19:6–9).

In verse 1 of the same chapter this scene is said to be in heaven. After this scene, John saw heaven opened and a rider, whose name is The Word of God, followed by the armies of heaven, go forth to smite the nations (Rev. 19:11–15). The marriage of the Lamb and the marriage supper shall therefore be in heaven before the closing conflict of the tribulation period.

Certain statements are made about the Church saints which are not said about any other group of saints. They are born of God and of the Spirit (John 1:13; 3:5). They are partakers of a divine nature (2 Pet. 1:4). They are heirs of God and joint heirs with Christ (Rom. 8:17). Of the Church Jesus said to His Father: "And the glory which thou gavest me I have given them" (John 17:22). All of these are conditions that must be true of the wife of the Lamb.

That the Old Testament saints are not the wife of the Lamb is seen in the statement by John the Baptist, the last of the Old Testament prophets, when he said: "The friend of the bridegroom, which standeth and heareth him, rejoiceth greatly because of the bridegroom's voice: this my joy therefore is fulfilled" (John 3:29). By this is seen that John considered himself as the friend of the bridegroom. That the Church shall have a higher position than the Old Testament heroes of faith is clearly taught in Hebrews 11:39–40. "And these . . . received not the promise: God having provided some better thing for us, that they without us should not be made perfect."

The saints that will come out of the tribulation cannot be the wife of the Lamb because they will "serve the Lamb day and night in his temple."

The fourth and last group of saints are the faithful of Israel passing through the tribulation. As these are on earth at the time of the marriage of the Lamb in heaven they cannot be the Lamb's wife.

Paul considered the Church as the future wife of Christ when he wrote: "For I am jealous over you with godly jealousy: for I have espoused you to one husband, that I may present you as a chaste virgin to Christ" (2 Cor. 11:2). Only the Church can be presented as a chaste virgin. God's chosen people, Israel, were by the prophets repeatedly spoken of as an adulteress. Even though she shall be restored, Israel can never be espoused to Christ as a chaste virgin.

In the following passage Paul clearly taught that the relationship of Christ to the Church is that of a husband to his wife:

"Husbands, love your wives, even as Christ also loved the church, and gave himself for it; that he might sanctify and cleanse it with the washing of water by the word, that he might present it to himself a glorious church, not having spot, or wrinkle, or any such thing; but that it should be holy and without blemish. So ought men to love their wives as their own bodies. He that loveth his wife loveth himself. For no man ever yet hated his own flesh; but nourisheth and cherisheth it, even as the Lord the church: for we are members of his body, of his flesh, and of his bones. For this cause shall a man leave his father and mother, and shall be joined unto his wife, and they two shall be one flesh. This is a great mystery: but I speak concerning Christ and the church" (Eph. 5:25–32).

Surely the Church shall not be on earth to pass through the judgment and wrath of God during the tribulation, the most awful days in human history. She shall then, in heaven, be elevated to the highest and most glorious position ever given to any of God's creatures. She shall become the bride of the Son of God.

CHAPTER 15

God's Vision for the Church

THE prophet of old said: "Where there is no vision, the people perish." This is a principle that governs all human life. The Church has been given the greatest vision ever given to any of God's creatures. This vision is, "the coming of our Lord Jesus Christ, and . . . our gathering together unto him."

To be occupied by this vision, to wait for its realization is to observe one of the three cardinal points of the believer's life under grace. Paul in writing to Titus set forth the three aspects of Christian life. "For the grace of God that bringeth salvation hath appeared to all men, teaching us that, denying ungodliness and worldly lusts, we should live soberly, righteously, and godly in this present world: looking for that blessed hope, and the glorious appearing of the great God and our Saviour Jesus Christ" (Titus 2:11–13).

According to this the *looking* for the glorious appearing of our Saviour Jesus Christ should be as important in the life of every member of the Church as to *deny* ungodliness and *live* righteously and godly. This great vision of the *glory* of His appearing should always be before every believer.

The same three points of Christian life are found in one of Paul's other letters: "Ye turned to God from idols to serve the living and true God; and to wait for his Son from heaven, whom he raised from the dead, even Jesus, which delivered us from the wrath to come" (1 Thess. 1:9–10).

The vision here is of the coming of the Son of God, with emphasis on that which He has already accomplished for those who look for Him. He who is to come from heaven is the same whom God raised from the dead, and who "delivered us from the wrath to come." In this passage the vision is enlarged to include deliverance *from* wrath. This is not deliverance through wrath. It cannot be by accident that deliverance from wrath through the death and resurrection of the Son of God is identified with waiting for Him.

When the Son of God bore our sins in His body on the tree "the sun was darkened." God hid His face from Him because of the sins He bore as is evidenced by His cry, "My God, my God, why hast thou forsaken me?" Because He went through that dark hour of separation from the Father and died and then rose again, the Church has been delivered from the gross darkness and the wrath to come during the tribulation period.

Because that which was accompanied by the death and resurrection of Christ cannot be a partial work, this must mean full and complete deliverance from all wrath. To hold that the Church shall pass through the tribulation, with its wrath, is to deny that He for whom the Church is waiting has delivered her from the wrath to come.

The wrath of the tribulation shall be the wrath of the Lamb. It shall be the wrath of Him who bore the sins of the Church in His body on the cross to deliver her from wrath. His wrath is for those who have rejected Him and all He did to deliver them from wrath. "He that believeth on the Son hath everlasting life: and he that believeth not the Son shall not see life; but the wrath of God abideth on him" (John 3:36).

One is forced to ask, How could the Lamb of God die and rise again to save the Church from wrath and then allow her to pass through the wrath that He shall pour upon those who reject Him? Such inconsistency might be possible in the thinking of men, but not in the acts of the Son of God.

The waiting for the Son of God from heaven, then, is accompanied by full assurance of deliverance from the tribulation with its wrath. That assurance becomes an essential part of the Church's vision.

A third passage again enlarges the vision by revealing the fact that glory shall come to every believer at the coming of the Lord Jesus Christ. "For our conversation [citizenship] is in heaven; from whence also we look for the Saviour, the Lord Jesus Christ: who shall change our vile body, that it may be fashioned like unto his glorious body" (Phil. 3:20-21).

"When Christ, who is our life, shall appear, then shall ye also appear with him in glory" (Col. 3:4). The trial of the believers' faith shall be "unto praise and honour and glory at the appearing of Jesus Christ" (1 Pet. 1:7). "And when the chief Shepherd shall appear, ye shall receive a crown of glory that fadeth not away" (1 Pet. 5:4).

The riches of God's glory shall be made known on the Church while He still endures with much long-suffering the vessels of wrath fitted for destruction (Rom. 9:22–23).

The third principle of Christian life, then, is to look for the glorious appearing of the great God and Saviour Jesus Christ. It is to wait for the Son of God from heaven in full assurance that He already has delivered from the wrath to come. It is to look for the Saviour Jesus Christ in expectation of sharing His glory. All that is implied by these statements belongs to God's vision for the Church. It is called the blessed hope of the Church.

When the apostles wanted to stir men up to patience, to labor, to hope, to endurance, to holiness, and other virtues, they spoke of this vision as an incentive. If this were not a perfect vision, if part thereof might not be realized, then God has set before the Church a partially false incentive. This cannot be admitted.

In the following verses the vision is used as an incentive to life.

"Let not your heart be troubled. . . . I go to prepare a place for you. . . . I will come again, and receive you unto myself; that where I am, there ye may be also" (John 14:1–3). "For the Lord himself shall descend from heaven . . . and the dead in

Christ shall rise first: then we which are alive and remain shall be caught up together with them in the clouds, to meet the Lord in the air: and so shall we ever be with the Lord. Wherefore comfort one another with these words" (1 Thess. 4:16–18). "Be ye also patient; stablish your hearts: for the coming of the Lord draweth nigh" (James 5:8). "When he shall appear, we shall be like him; for we shall see him as he is. And every man that hath this hope in him purifieth himself, even as he is pure" (1 John 3:2–3).

It is important that any vision be not blurred to be a real incentive to life. If anything beclouds the vision, its effectiveness becomes restricted. It may even be completely lost. To teach that a period of tribulation and wrath, such as the world has never before experienced, lies ahead before the realization of the vision is to take the eyes of the Church off the vision and center them on that period. Thus the vision becomes dimmed and its purpose as an incentive to purity, to patience, to steadfastness, and to other aspects of Christian life is lessened. The comfort and blessedness of Christ's return is left without point.

In all passages which mention the coming or the appearing of the Lord Jesus Christ, the words used imply imminence. That is imminent which can happen at any time without the intervention of some other event. Not one passage can be found that tells of some coming event that must precede the Lord's return for the Church.

This absence of mention of any event to precede the coming of the Lord takes on importance when it is observed that God has given Israel a vision of a glorious kingdom on earth. But it is repeatedly said that Israel must first go through a time of great trouble.

It is impossible for any believer to say or even feel, "The Lord might come today," unless the Lord's coming is imminent. If the mid-tribulationists should be right, three and a half years must intervene between the signing of a covenant with Israel and the rapture. If the post-tribulationists should be right it must be seven years.

But God always refers to an imminent coming of His Son from heaven. Yes, He may come today.

"Surely, I come quickly." "Even so, come, Lord Jesus."

CHAPTER 16

Introduction to Part Two

BECAUSE many persons have been disturbed by the more or less recent writings and teachings of mid- and post-tribulationists it has seemed helpful to call attention to some errors contained in their arguments. It is not the purpose here to call attention to all such errors, but merely to show how some of the important arguments are not valid in the light of the Scriptures. A considerable number of other arguments have been examined and found just as vulnerable as those that are here presented, but space does not permit discussion of all, nor is anything to be gained thereby. The proof of the pre-tribulation view is in the Scriptures, not in the refutation of the arguments offered in support of other views.

That which is here presented is therefore not offered as proof of the pre-tribulation view, but rather to show the weakness of the post-tribulation view and the untenableness of many of the essential arguments offered in support of that view. The proof has already been given in Part I, but it is often helpful to dispose of erroneous ideas in order to prepare the mind for that which is true. It should be pointed out that much that is offered as proof is no proof at all. It will be helpful to point out the deficiencies of some of these so-called proofs.

Many, if not all, passages used to support the post-tribulation view are subject to more than one interpretation. The post-tribulation writer presents the interpretation which supports his view. There is no criticism of this, but instead of supporting his interpretation by quoting other Scripture passages he supports it by the opinions of "great scholars." With due respect for these scholars, their opinions are not the Word of God. These corroborative opinions might easily be influenced by the view held by such persons. It follows that any conclusions based on such opinions are only on the authority of man. This is true on whatever side of the controversy the opinions are expressed. Always be on guard against interpretations of doubtful passages that are not supported by other Scripture.

Ridicule of an opponent or his arguments is frequently and effectively used in argumentation but there is no proof in ridicule and surely it is entirely out of place in discussing the doctrines of the Church. It also displays passion on the part of the one who uses it and a lack of unbiased thinking. All such statements should be completely ignored as having no weight.

Questions that are asked and not answered cannot be admitted as proof. The following is typical of questions found frequently enough to justify comment. "If the Church is permitted to remain in the world today while Jewry is undergoing a terrible tribulation in Europe and elsewhere, why is there any incongruity in the thought of the Church being in the world during the Tribulation when Israel will suffer again?" There is absolutely no proof. This question arose in the mind of a man and unless the reader is well versed in the Scriptures the answer will also be according to human reasoning and not according to the Word of God. All such questions must be completely disregarded.

Space does not permit the discussion of arguments of this type, nor is it necessary because the reader will be able to recognize them for what they are.

These pages are written with a deep consciousness that there have been in the past and now there are godly men who love the appearing of the Lord, who have consecrated their lives to the spreading of the Gospel of the grace of God, and have given unstintingly of themselves, who hold views differing from those here presented. It is hoped that nothing herein will in the least be taken to reflect upon them personally.

No names of present or recent writers are mentioned in the following pages to make the discussion as impersonal as possible. That which is attacked is not the individuals but the arguments that are set forth by these persons. The purpose is to expose error, not to discredit men.

Because the Christian public of the present time is confronted by the more recent writings of mid- and post-tribulationists, it is well to confine the following comments to such writings.

CHAPTER 17

The Elect and the Saints of the End Time

THE ELECT

THE use of the word *elect* three times in Matthew 24 is offered as evidence that the Church will pass through the tribulation. In support of this it is said: "One of the common words in the Epistles for the saved of this dispensation is elect." This statement is true but this use in the Epistles does not prove that this is the meaning when *elect* is used in Matthew and in the other Synoptic Gospels.

But it is also true that Paul applied the word *election* to Israel three times in Romans 11:5, 7, 28. He also used it of Jacob, from whom all Israel has descended, in 9:11. Thus the Epistles do not support the exclusive use of *elect* for the Church. Another writer has said: "Of the sixteen occurrences of the term elect in the New Testament, one refers to certain angels, another refers to Christ and the other fourteen very obviously refer to the Church or Christians. To make the term refer to any others requires 'special pleading.'" This statement is *not* true. Only of seven occurrences can it be said that they obviously refer to the Church. Of the other seven, three are the ones in Matthew 24:22, 24, 31, the same that this writer is trying to apply to the Church. Three more are in Mark 13:20, 22, 27

recording the same discourse of Jesus as is found in
Matthew and one in Luke 18:7 is also related to the
coming of the Son of man. A statement like the
above is not only void of proof, but altogether mis-
leading.

It has also been said that there is no reason for
denying that the elect on earth during the tribulation are the Church of Christ. This statement be-
trays a serious lack of knowledge of the point at issue.

The word *elect* is applied to Israel as well as the
Church and Israel is mentioned by name as being in
the tribulation, while the Church is never so mentioned. This alone should cause anyone to hesitate
to make such a statement. But additional Scriptural
evidence to show that the elect of Matthew 24 belong to Israel is not hard to find.

The fact that Jesus in verse 15 mentioned the
abomination of desolation spoken of by Daniel
shows that He was speaking of something that concerns Israel. He also said: "Then let them which be
in Judea flee into the mountains." And again: "But
pray ye that your flight be not in winter, neither on
the sabbath day." These statements were addressed
to Jews. The elect mentioned in verses 22 and 24
must be the same people to whom He spoke. These
elect are *obviously* not the Church but Israel. It
should also be remembered that the seventieth week
of Israel is the tribulation period. During that time
Israel is again recognized by God as His chosen people just as they were before and during the first

sixty-nine of the seventy weeks determined upon them. That qualifies Israel as God's elect during the tribulation and it is for them that those days are shortened.

The elect of verse 31 are to be gathered by the *angels* "from the four winds, from one end of heaven to the other." When the Church shall be caught up to be with the Lord, *the Lord Himself* and no other descends from heaven, as explained in Chapter 3.

Furthermore the description of this gathering of the elect is in harmony with the gathering of Israel as foretold by Moses. "If any of thine be driven out unto the outmost parts of heaven, from thence will the LORD thy God gather thee, and from thence will he fetch thee" (Deut. 30:4).

But this does not exhaust the evidence that the elect of Matthew 24:31 belong to Israel. Isaiah lends his voice in support of this view. He prophesied that when the iniquity of Jacob shall have been purged ". . . it shall come to pass that . . . ye shall be gathered one by one, O ye children of Israel. And it shall come to pass in that day, that the great trumpet shall be blown, and they shall come . . . and shall worship the LORD in the holy mount at Jerusalem" (Isaiah 27:9, 12–13). It is at the end of the seventieth week of Israel which has been seen to be the end of the tribulation that the iniquity of Jacob shall have been purged. It is then that the Son of man shall send His angels with "a great sound of a trumpet" to gather His elect. Israel shall be gathered by the blowing of a great trumpet. The elect are gathered at a great sound of a trumpet and both at the same time. Is it not obvious that Israel and the elect are the same people?

Again speaking of this restoration of Israel, Isaiah said: "And I will bring forth a seed out of Jacob, and out of Judah an inheritor of my mountains: and mine elect shall inherit it, and my servants shall dwell there" (65:9). "They shall not build, and another inhabit; they shall not plant, and another eat: for as the days of a tree are the days of my people, and mine elect shall long enjoy the work of their hands" (v. 22). These elect are Israel and they shall belong to that period of time that will be brought in by the coming of the Son of man with power and great glory.

In the face of all this evidence that Israel must be the elect mentioned in Matthew 24, how can anyone be bold to say that these elect are the Church and that without offering a single Scripture passage to support the contention?

The error here, as is true so often in post-tribulation arguments, is due to a failure to recognize the distinctively Jewish aspect of the passage in question.

THE SAINTS

The fact that saints are seen in the tribulation is also offered as a proof that the Church will pass through that time of unequaled terror. It is said that the word *saint* in Revelation always applies to the Church and as proof most verses in which that word is used are quoted. Space does not permit discussion of all these passages nor is it necessary. One statement alone shows the shallowness of thinking behind this argument.

It is said: "Then in terms as clear and explicit as language can find—at XIX 8–9 . . . —the *saints* are identified on the very Day of the Lord with the Church, the Bride of Christ of this Dispensation." Everyone accepting the pre-tribulation view is very happy to acknowledge that in this passage the word *saint* does apply to the Church and that for a very good reason. Verse one of this chapter places the scene here described in heaven. Therefore the saints, the Church, here spoken of must be in heaven. That is where the Church according to the pre-tribulation view must be during the tribulation. It is, however, not agreed that the statement of that writer that this is "on the very Day of the Lord" is correct because he holds that the day of the Lord is the single event when the Son of man comes in the clouds of heaven. The day of the Lord is an extended period of time covering many years. This scene in heaven will come before the final battle of Armageddon which is a part of the tribulation. Yes, this verse shows that the Church is in heaven and not on earth during the tribulation. It would have been better for the post-tribulation cause to quote a verse that shows clearly that the saints on earth during the tribulation are members of the Church. But this was not done. Why? Because no such verse can be found.

Who then are the saints that will be on earth during the tribulation? In seeking an answer it must be remembered first, that the word *saint,* both in the Old and New Testaments, means 'set apart, separated, holy.' Second, the tribulation corresponds to the day of Jacob's trouble and the seventieth week of Israel. Throughout the Old Testament the word *saint* is applied to Israelites. The distinctive characteristic that God demanded of Israel was that they should be a separated people. Third, the presence on earth during the tribulation of 144,000 Israelites set apart as servants of God is clearly taught (Rev. 7:3–8). Fourth, an innumerable group of persons saved during the tribulation shall be before the throne of God and serve Him day and night. These cannot, as post-tribulationists claim, be the Church because the Bride in her heavenly position will not *serve* God. In the Upper Room where He clearly taught Church truth, Jesus said to His disciples: "Henceforth I call you not servants . . . but I have called you friends" (John 15:15).

Here then are seen two separate groups, both are 'set apart' by God for His service. They are saints. They are also said to be on the earth during the tribulation. In view of this, how can anyone declare that the word *saint* in Revelation always applies to the Church.

Just as with the word *elect,* there is definite evidence to show that the word *saint* is used of Israel in Revelation. In Chapter 13 it is said that a beast shall arise having seven heads and ten horns, and he shall receive the worship of the world. To him shall be given a mouth that shall speak great things and power to continue forty-two months, or three and one-half years. "And it was given unto him to make war with the saints, and to overcome them" (v. 7). Daniel in Chapter 7 tells of the same beast with ten horns. The little horn of this beast had a mouth that spake very great things, and the same "made war with the saints, and prevailed against them" (v. 21). "And he shall speak great words against the most High, and shall wear out the saints of the most High . . . and they shall be given into his hand until a time and times and the dividing of time" (v. 25). This has been interpreted as three and one-half years and corresponds to the forty-two months of the duration of the power of the beast in Revelation 13. "And the kingdom . . . shall be given to the people of the saints of the most High" (v. 27).

That which Daniel saw is identical with that which John saw and both belong to the last half of the tribulation. The saints of whom Daniel wrote are those of his people Israel. That being so, those of whom John wrote must also belong to Israel.

Here the saints of Israel are seen on earth during the tribulation. But previously the saints, the bride of the Lamb, were seen in heaven before the closing conflict of the tribulation. Thus it is seen that the use of the word *saint* in Revelation is not, as is claimed in support of the post-tribulation view, a proof that the Church shall be on earth and pass through the tribulation. In fact, it supports the pre-tribulation view and is in perfect harmony with arguments in support of that view.

CHAPTER 18

The Parousia According to the Post-Tribulation View

THE post-tribulation view requires that the parousia must come after the tribulation because 1 Thessalonians 4:15–17 unmistakably declares that the dead in Christ shall be raised first and the Church raptured at the parousia. Because the Son of man shall come on the clouds of heaven with power and great glory *after* the tribulation, every effort possible has been made to identify that event as the parousia.

In support of this view it has been argued that the word *parousia* has the technical meaning of a sovereign coming to his subjects. This claim is seen in the following statement: *"Parousia* was everywhere used in the sense of the *arrival* or *coming* of kings and rulers on a visit to a town. How appropriate to the arrival of our Saviour-God, Jesus Christ, when He comes in triumph to rescue His afflicted people, and establish the kingly rule of God." Yes, how appropriate! *But why did Jesus not use the word parousia when He foretold His coming in the clouds of heaven?*

Why try so desperately to force the parousia into Matthew 24:30 where the divine Author of the Bible does not use it? Only because that is the one

verse that tells of a coming of the Son of man after
the tribulation, and the post-tribulation view rests
very heavily on the interpretation of that verse as
the parousia.

Of the twenty-four times the word is used in the
New Testament, not once is it used to denote the
coming of the Lord as King. It would seem that the
use of the word in the Bible is of far greater importance to indicate its Biblical meaning than is its use
in old papyri. Furthermore, even in the papyri it is
not always so used.

Again, 2 Thessalonians 2:8 is supposed to teach
that the parousia shall be after the tribulation because the man of sin is brought to nought by the
parousia. It is said of 2 Thessalonians 2: ". . . this
very chapter shows that the antichrist is slain by
Christ at His coming (*Parousia*, verse 8)." This is,
however, as shown in Chapter 9, not by the parousia but by the manifestation of the parousia. The
two words "manifestation of" are ignored in order to
make this passage prove a post-tribulation parousia.

One wonders why a writer, who devotes a chapter
to show that the parousia shall be after the tribulation and pretends to discuss the subject with com-
pleteness, fails to discuss Matthew 24:37–39 where
the word *parousia* is used twice; although he does
discuss the less important use of the word in verses
3 and 27. As shown in Chapter 8, the parousia of
the Son of man, as described in Matthew 24:37–39,
must be before the destruction begins and therefore
must precede the tribulation. This passage alone

completely contradicts the argument for a post-tribulation parousia unless one is willing to admit that
the parousia occurs twice. This possibility the writer
quoted above completely rejects.

Special effort is made to show that the essential
meaning of the word *parousia* is merely an arrival
and thereby limits the parousia of the Lord to the
one event, the coming in the clouds of heaven. In
support of this it is said, "Of particular interest is
2 Cor. 7. 'But God who comforts the dejected comforted me by the *arrival* of Titus. Yes, and by more
than his *arrival*' (6–7). According to the conjecture
of Wieseler, cited by Weymouth, Titus walked in as
Paul was writing. This cheered the Apostle, as did
the report he gave. This one passage completely
demonstrates that *arrival* is a fundamental meaning
of *Parousia;* Paul was comforted by the arrival, and
the subsequent intercourse." Here the *conjecture* of
Wieseler is made to demonstrate completely that a
fundamental meaning of parousia is an arrival.
When did it become permissible to interpret the
Bible by the conjectures of men?

Furthermore, this writer seemed to forget that he
had pressed the meaning of the word as being "the
arrival of kings and rulers, or the visit following."
Does not the "visit following" require a subsequent
presence with? It certainly does. The coming in the
clouds of heaven is not the arrival aspect of the parousia. It may be an event during the subsequent
presence or an entirely separate coming.

Again, being possessed with the need of insisting

upon the coming in the clouds of heaven as the parousia, the idea of a parousia that will be secret to
the world as taught by some pre-tribulationists is
denounced. This denunciation is supposed to be the
death knell to the pre-tribulation view. It is said,
"That the Lord's *parousia* would not be secret, but
in manifest glory, for all shall see the Lord coming
in the clouds of heaven." Not one verse in the Bible
in which the word parousia is used will support this
statement.

Inasmuch as the Divine Author of the Bible did
not see fit to use the word *parousia* in Matthew
24:30, no man has a right to force that meaning into
that passage and then argue from that verse about
the nature of the parousia. Unfortunately, the average reader has no way of knowing that the "coming"
of that verse is not the parousia and is therefore misled by all of these arguments which attempt to locate
the parousia of the Lord in that verse.

Apart from the fact that a secret parousia disqualifies Matthew 24:30 as evidence of a post-tribulation
parousia, what difference does secrecy make as to the
time thereof? Absolutely none. Therefore, the only
reason for denying the secrecy is to hold tenaciously
to this verse as a most important proof of the post-
tribulation view.

But there is evidence that as far as the world is
concerned the parousia will be secret. When the
Egyptians pursued the Israelites across the Red Sea,
were they aware of the presence of the Lord in the

dark cloud between them and the Israelites? Surely not.

At the parousia of the Son of man (Matt. 24:37–39) no manifest glory is seen. The inhabitants of the earth will not be aware of His coming before the destruction strikes them and nothing in the words of Jesus indicates that they will know who caused the destruction to come.

Paul, in 1 Thessalonians 4:15–17 and 5:2–3, related the coming of the day of the Lord to the parousia of the Lord. That day will come as a thief in the night. The essential element in the coming of a thief is secrecy, therefore, the coming of that day and of Him who brings in that day must also be secret. No manifest glory is seen in that passage.

The fact that the parousia of the Lord is veiled in the clouds until the manifestation, yes, the shining forth thereof, brings to nought the wicked is additional evidence of an arrival that is secret to the world. It shall be after this *manifestation* of the parousia that the tribes of the earth shall see Him coming in the clouds of heaven.

To say that the Lord had told His disciples "that the *Lord's Parousia* would not be secret, but in manifest glory, for all should see the *Lord* coming on the clouds of heaven" is a misstatement. It is not true. If the Lord had intended this verse to describe His parousia the Holy Spirit would have led Matthew to use that word.

When Jesus did speak of His parousia as recorded

in the same chapter, verses 37–39, no reference was made to His being seen by the tribes of the earth. There He represents Himself in the role of the Son of man, that is, the one to whom all judgment has been given, coming to bring judgment upon the unsuspecting world. That is just what will happen during the tribulation. At no place is any word said about the world seeing Him at that time.

If the coming in the clouds of heaven were the parousia, a most serious contradiction would be seen within the space of ten verses of Matthew 24, and that in the words of the Son of God.

Why will a post-tribulationist go to such extremes as the above to read the parousia into Matthew 24:30? Because that is the capstone of his entire argument for the post-tribulation view. Upon the parousia hangs the time of the resurrection of the dead in Christ and the rapture of the Church, as is undeniably taught in 1 Thessalonians 4:15–17.

Speaking of a secret rapture which is directly related to the secret parousia it has been said: "It is as pure a myth as ever entered the brain of man."

The thought that an innumerable body of sleeping saints shall rise at the coming of Christ as told in 1 Thessalonians 4:15–17 without making any impression on the world is ridiculed. But why not? All these saints shall be raised with bodies like unto the glorious body of Christ when He arose from the grave. There is no record that He was seen after He arose by anyone except believers. Christ's body passed through closed doors. His body was invisible

except at times when He *showed* Himself to witnesses chosen by God.

And what of the living saints? They shall also be
changed in the twinkling of an eye into bodies like
Christ's. Of course, the world will know that something has happened because all believers shall suddenly disappear from the presence of the unsaved
with whom they are when that moment comes. But
to insist that the world will witness the catching up
of the believers in the clouds of heaven is to disre-
gard the fact that the natural eyes of men are not
made to see spiritual things. Remember the bodies
that are taken up on the clouds do not react to
gravity. In its final analysis the error of this post-
tribulation argument is to ascribe to the glorified
bodies of believers the qualities of the natural bodies
and give to the natural bodies of the unsaved, who
are left, the faculties of the spiritual. An argument
such as this might be expected from the world, but
not from one who is a member of the new creation
in Christ. This is *reasoning* from the natural point
of view concerning things spiritual.

It is further claimed that the parousia shall be at
the day of the Lord. It has been said: "At 2 Thess.
2:1 it [i.e., the parousia] is mentioned with the as-
sembling of the Elect as one of two events charac-
terizing the day of the Lord and requiring to be
fulfilled before anyone could say, 'the Day of the
Lord has come.' " By limiting the day of the Lord
to the one event when the Son of man shall come
in the clouds of heaven with power and great glory

that day is made to come after the tribulation. As has been shown in Chapter 4, the day of the Lord will cover a long period of years, and therefore is not confined to one event.

A summary of the above post-tribulation arguments will show the falsity of the entire structure of that view.

1. Discoveries of science are said to show that the word *parousia* applies to the coming of kings. Therefore, the parousia of the Lord will be when He shall come with power and great glory. The Bible does not teach this.

2. The wicked, it is said, shall be brought to nought by the parousia. The Bible says this shall be by the *manifestation of* the parousia.

3. One of the clearest passages of the Bible about the time of the parousia, one that unquestionably places it before the tribulation, is completely omitted from a discussion that is represented as being complete.

4. By using the *conjecture* of a fallible human being, an effort is made to give the impression that the essential meaning of parousia is merely an arrival and not an extended period of time.

5. Denouncing and ridiculing the idea of a secret parousia and offering a false statement of what the Lord told His disciples about the parousia.

6. By teaching that the parousia shall be at the day of the Lord and then limiting that day to a single event that shall transpire after the tribulation.

In view of the above, it is pertinent to ask: What has the post-tribulation view to offer to commend itself when one of its most ardent adherents of the present generation has no better arguments to offer in its support?

CHAPTER 19

The Post-Tribulation View of the Rapture and the Day of the Lord

ACCORDING to the post-tribulation view the rapture of the Church will be when the Son of man comes in the clouds of heaven with power and great glory, and sends His angels to gather the elect from one end of heaven to the other.

It has been said: "When He comes according to 1 Thess. 4:13–17 and Matt. 24:31, He is on His way to earth to establish the Messianic Kingdom. But before the blow falls upon the ungodly, the Elect are gathered from one end of heaven to the other to meet the approaching Lord. They meet the Lord in the air and follow in His train."

By this statement, 1 Thessalonians 4:13–17 and Matthew 24:31 are said to describe the same event. As 1 Thessalonians 4:15–17 describes the rapture, then, so also must Matthew 24:31. In fact, that is the verse upon which the post-tribulation view rests heavily. If this verse can be shown to be the rapture, the post-tribulationists are right.

In Chapter 18 it is shown that their arguments to locate the parousia at Matthew 24:30 are not in accordance with the Scriptures, but rather a perversion of them. It is also shown in Chapter 17 that the word *elect* used in this verse 30 does not apply to the Church, but to Israel. Therefore, those spoken of there are not the Church, as is the case in 1 Thessalonians 4:15–17.

The rapture, according to Paul, shall come before "the blow falls upon the ungodly," as is acknowledged in the above quotation. But the gathering of the elect of verse 31 shall be after the blow has fallen upon the ungodly. The context clearly states that the event in Matthew shall transpire after the tribulation.

The following post-tribulation explanation of the rapture is supposed to support the contention that Matthew 24:31 describes the rapture. It is said that when the Son of man comes in the clouds of heaven the Church is caught up to meet Him in the air. As the Church meets Christ she turns about and returns with Him to the earth to establish His kingdom. An illustration by Chrysostom, one of the early Church Fathers, has been quoted in support of this view of the rapture. "If He is to descend, for what purpose shall we be caught away? To honor us. For so, when a king is entering a city, those in honorable station go forth to meet him, but the criminals await the judge within, and when a fond father arrives, the children, worthy of the name, are taken out in a chariot, to see and caress him, but unoffending domestics remain within."

How beautiful and convincing if it only were a true illustration! But the members of the Church, illustrated by the worthy children, are not at home on the earth nor are they in an "honorable" station on earth. Their home and citizenship are in the many mansions of the Father's house to which Jesus promised to bring them. Furthermore, the Lord is not coming home when He descends from heaven to take the Church unto Himself. He shall leave His home to meet the Church and bring her to His home.

A better interpretation of the rapture is one that is in harmony with the Bible illustration thereof. It is always better to find the Bible verification of any interpretation of the Scriptures. Abraham is a type of God the Father. His servant, whom he sent to find a bride for his son, is a type of the Holy Spirit. Isaac, the son, is a type of Christ. When the servant returned with Rebekah, Isaac went out into the field in the eventide and met them. Did Isaac continue on and bring Rebekah back to Mesopotamia? He did not. The Bible says, "And Isaac brought her into his mother Sarah's tent, and took Rebekah, and she became his wife; and he loved her" (Gen. 24:67). So when the Holy Spirit who shall be taken out of the way before the man of sin is revealed, leaves the earth with the Church, they shall be met in the air by the Lord as He descends from heaven. Then He will escort the Church into the many mansions of the Father's house, and there she will become His bride.

Chrysostom and those who so confidently quote him, have overlooked the fact that the marriage of the Lamb and the bride, the Church, will take place in heaven before the final great conflict on earth, before the tribulation has come to an end. This completely nullifies the post-tribulation claim that the rapture is in Matthew 24:31.

The two passages describe two separate and distinct events. In the first, the Lord Himself descends from heaven to raise the dead in Christ and catch up the Church. In the second, angels are sent out to gather the elect (elsewhere shown to be Israel) from the four winds. In the first the Lord comes with the "trump of God." In the second, angels are sent with a trumpet. In the first only the Church, God's heavenly people, is seen. In the second only the tribes of the earth are seen. The first, according to its context (1 Thess. 5:2–3), shall come before the coming of the day of the Lord with its sudden destruction. The second event shall be after the sudden destruction of the tribulation. The first culminates in the Church being forever with the Lord. The second issues in the establishment of a kingdom upon earth.

But the post-tribulation view requires even more distortion of Matthew 24:30–31 than the above to prove a post-tribulation rapture. It is held that the single event recorded in this passage is the day of the Lord. It has been freely admitted that the rapture will take place at the day of the Lord. Then, in order to uphold the post-tribulation view, it becomes necessary to limit the day of the Lord to this one event which will come after the tribulation. It is true that the coming of the Son of man in the clouds of heaven is an event of the day of the Lord but according to Peter that day is a period of a thousand years.

To hold this post-tribulation view one must shut the eyes completely to a large body of truth relative to the day of the Lord as foretold by the Old Testament prophets. Much of this cannot possibly come to pass after the Son of man shall come in the clouds of heaven.

Joel said of the day of the Lord: "As a destruction from the Almighty shall it come" (1:15). Surely this does not take place when the Sun of Righteousness shall rise with healing in His wings. Again Joel described the day of the Lord as "a day of darkness and gloominess, a day of clouds and of thick darkness." That does not describe the coming of the Son of man in *great glory*.

Amos also said: "Shall not the day of the LORD be darkness, and not light? even very dark, and no brightness in it?" (5:20). Surely this cannot be the event recorded in Matthew 24:30. Zephaniah said: "That day is a day of wrath, a day of trouble and distress, a day of wasteness and desolation, a day of darkness and gloominess, a day of clouds and thick darkness" (1:15). Isaiah said: "Behold, the day of the LORD cometh, cruel both with wrath and fierce anger" (13:9).

These and many other things foretold by the prophets cannot be harmonized with the event recorded by Matthew nor can it be said that they can come to pass after that time because that coming of the Son of man shall be to restore and to set up His kingdom in which peace and righteousness shall rule.

As shown in Chapter 6, all these things must happen during the tribulation. It was also shown that the day of the Lord begins when the tribulation begins.

Paul, as has already been explained (see Chapter 4), said the day of the Lord shall come with sudden destruction "when they shall say, Peace and safety." This is the time to which he relates the rapture, and not to the coming of the Son of man in the clouds of heaven.

Here again is seen a distortion of the Scriptures in an effort to establish the post-tribulation view.

CHAPTER 20

The Parables of Matthew Thirteen

THE WHEAT AND THE TARES

THE parable of the wheat and the tares, as recorded in Matthew 13:24–30, with the explanation that Jesus gave thereof, as recorded in verses
36–43, is offered as a proof that the Church shall pass
through the tribulation.

Verse 30 is offered as conclusive evidence. It
reads: "Let both grow together until the harvest:
and in the time of harvest I will say to the reapers,
Gather ye together first the tares, and bind them in
bundles to burn them: but gather the wheat into my
barn."

It is generally accepted that the parables of Matthew 13 are prophetic of the time intervening between the rejection, by the Jews, of Christ and His
return in glory. There seems to be no valid reason
to question this view. It is also evident that this
parable relates the harvest to the very end of that
period.

The decisive words in this parable are said to be,
"Gather ye together first the tares . . . but gather
the wheat into my barn." It is asserted that the
"wheat" represents the whole company of Christians
won by the Gospel, and that the "tares" represent
the mass of mere professors in Christendom. The

former class is said to be the sons of God; the latter the sons of the evil one.

This takes place at the very end of this age and the bringing in of the wheat into the barn follows the destruction of the wicked. This must place the event at the time that Christ comes to set up His kingdom. It is therefore held to be impossible for the Church to be raptured at a time, seven years, more or less, earlier. A pre-tribulation rapture is therefore held to be impossible. It is said: "Read naturally the 'Parable of the Tares' spells midnight to the new theories and the Second Coming," by which is meant the pre-tribulation rapture. No evidence is offered to show that this ingathering is the same as the one Paul calls "our gathering together unto the Lord."

There is, however, considerable evidence that the rapture of the Church and that spoken of in this parable are not the same but entirely different events.

Notice carefully that reapers are sent to "gather the wheat into my barn." In verses 38 and 39 Jesus explained that the good seed is the children of the kingdom and the reapers are the angels. Here, then, is a picture of angels gathering in the children of the kingdom into the kingdom.

Compare with this the description of the rapture: "For the Lord himself shall descend from heaven . . . then we . . . shall be caught up together . . . to meet the Lord in the air." Notice that the "Lord himself" in person comes to receive His body, which is His Church, unto Himself. When the body, the Church, is to be united with the head, Christ, angels are not sufficient for that mission. When Christ presents the Church unto Himself, a glorious Church (Eph. 5:25–27), no angel is worthy of escorting the Church to Him. He, Himself, and no other comes for her.

There is more to indicate that this parable does not apply to the Church. Jesus said: "The good seed are the children of the kingdom." This term is never in the Bible applied to the Church. Believers of this age of grace are called children of light (John 12:36; 1 Thess. 5:5) and children of God (Rom. 8:16, 21; Gal. 3:26; 1 John 3:10; 5:2). But Jesus in Matthew 8:10–13 applied the name *children of the kingdom* to Israel. Referring to the faith of the centurion (Matt. 8:5–13) He said: "Verily I say unto you, I have not found so great faith, no, not in Israel, and I say unto you, That many shall come from the east and west, and shall sit down with Abraham, and Isaac, and Jacob, in the kingdom of heaven. But the children of the kingdom shall be cast out into outer darkness" (vs. 10–12). These that are cast out are those of Israel who rejected Jesus.

When Peter said to Jesus, "Behold, we have forsaken all, and followed thee; what shall we have therefore?" Jesus answered, "Verily I say unto you, That ye which have followed me, in the regeneration when the Son of man shall sit in the throne of his glory, ye also shall sit upon twelve thrones, judging the twelve tribes of Israel" (Matt. 19:27–29). Here the twelve tribes of Israel are seen in the kingdom. They must be the children of the kingdom.

The question now arises, Does the Bible tell of anything that shall transpire between the time that the Son of man was on the cross and when He shall come with power and great glory in the clouds of heaven that can be called a sowing of the children of the kingdom in the field, that is the world?

Yes, it does. It is found in Revelation 7:3-4, where "servants of our God" are sealed in their foreheads before any hurt comes to the earth, or the sea, or the trees. These servants of God, numbering 144,000, are "of all the tribes of the children of Israel." There will be 12,000 of each tribe. Beyond doubt these are descendants of Jacob, whom God renamed Israel, because all the twelve tribes are mentioned by name.

Here, then, is a group of God's servants to carry on His work in the world during the tribulation period. They are the good seed, the children of the kingdom that are sown in the field. There is no other group of persons mentioned in the Bible that can be said to fit into the parable as do these.

This identifies the seed sowing of this parable with the tribulation period.

If the seed is the children of the kingdom, then the harvest must be children of the kingdom. It follows that the harvest is the ingathering of Israel and not the Church.

The time of "the harvest is the end of the world." "The reapers are the angels." The angels reap both the tares and the wheat. Throughout the tribulation period angels are the instruments used of God to pour out His judgments and wrath upon the world.

This fulfills Jesus' explanation, "The Son of man shall send forth his angels, and they shall gather out of his kingdom all things that offend, and them which do iniquity" (Matt. 13:41).

The angels also reap the wheat. This follows the reaping of the tares. Jesus told of this reaping in Matthew 24:29–31: "Immediately after the tribulation of those days shall the sun be darkened, and the moon shall not give her light, and the stars shall fall from heaven, and the powers of the heavens shall be shaken: and then shall appear the sign of the Son of man in heaven: and then shall all of the tribes of the earth mourn, and they shall see the Son of man coming in the clouds of heaven with power and great glory. And he shall send his angels with a great sound of a trumpet, and they shall gather together his elect from the four winds, from one end of heaven to the other." Here are seen angels as the reapers gathering Israel, God's elect people, from the four winds after the tares have been burned, after they have "gathered out of his kingdom all things that offend, and them which do iniquity."

Even more can be said to show that the parable of the wheat and the tares is in no wise related to the Church.

The meaning of gathering the wheat "into my barn" is found in Jesus' explanation of the parable. He said: "Then shall the righteous shine forth as the sun in the kingdom of their Father." It is into the kingdom that the reapers shall gather Israel from the four winds. The Church cannot be gathered into the kingdom at the end of the age because she is already in. All believers have been delivered from the power of darkness and translated into the kingdom of God's dear Son (Col. 1:13). This ingathering into the kingdom has been going on for more than nineteen hundred years. When the Church is gathered unto Christ it shall be into the mansions of the Father's house (John 14:2).

If this parable is studied together with the first parable given at the same time, considerable light will be cast upon its meaning. Both parables are about seed sowing, but the seed is not the same in both. According to Jesus' own explanation, the seed in the first is the Word; in the second it is persons, the children of the kingdom. In the first the seed is sown in the hearts of individual men. In the second it is sown in the world.

The program for the Church age is, as Paul wrote to Timothy, "Preach the word." The responsibility of the individual person is to receive the word into his heart to believe it. "For with the heart man believeth unto righteousness" (Rom. 10:10). The word thus sown produces fruit. This fruit is those that are born again. "Being born again, not of corruptible seed, but of incorruptible, by the word of God, which liveth and abideth forever" (1 Pet. 1:23).

It must be significant that all of the seven parables of Matthew 13 with the *exception of the first,* are introduced by the words, "The kingdom of heaven is like unto." It could not be by accident that Jesus omitted these words from the first parable and

that its first words simply are, "A sower went forth
to sow." This sets the first parable off from the others
in a class by itself. Here is a seed-sowing that is not
said to be likened unto the kingdom of heaven as is
the sowing of the second parable. Hence two different sowings are seen in these parables.

It is evident, then, that the first parable describes
conditions during the present Church age, and the
second that which shall take place during the tribulation period, when a remnant of 144,000 of Israel
shall become God's servants upon the earth. A
remnant of Israel is here seen as God's servants min-
istering to the world just prior to the bringing in of
righteousness. This is in perfect harmony with the
words spoken to Daniel by Gabriel: "Seventy weeks
are determined upon thy people and upon thy holy
city, to finish the transgression, and to make an end
of sins, and to make reconciliation for iniquity, and
to bring in everlasting righteousness, and to seal up
the vision and prophecy, and to anoint the most
holy."

Of these seventy weeks sixty-nine had transpired,
as has previously been explained, when Messiah was
cut off (i.e., crucified). The seventieth week is
marked by a covenant made with Israel. It is broken
in the middle of the week, by cessation of the obla-
tion, and the overspreading of the abomination of
desolation (Dan. 9:24–27). Jesus in the Olivet Discourse clearly identified the "abomination of desolation," spoken of by Daniel the prophet, with the
tribulation period preceding the coming of the Son

of man in the clouds of heaven with power and great glory.

Between the sixty-ninth week of Daniel's prophecy, which ended with the crucifixion of the Messiah, and the seventieth week, when God shall again reckon time according to Israel, is a long period of time. It has already lasted more than nineteen hundred years. It will close when the covenant with Israel is made. During this intervening period God the sower has been sowing His seed, even His Word, in the hearts of men. He will continue to do so until He sows 144,000 of the twelve tribes of Israel in the world. Then the intervening period with its sowing shall cease. The work of taking out of the world a people for His name's sake will then be finished. The Church is ready to be raptured when the seventieth week of Daniel (the tribulation) is ready to come upon the dwellers of the earth. Christ's body is ready to be received into heaven before the day of Jacob's trouble, the day of wrath, comes upon an unbelieving world.

Not one, but two separate and distinct parables are needed to present God's seed-sowing from the time the Son of man was lifted up on the cross until He shall come in glory. The first covers the Church age and the second the seven-year, unfulfilled, period of God's recognition of Israel as His servants on earth after the Church period is over.

In these two parables is found no argument for a post-tribulation rapture but when the first ends and the second is about to begin there is provided a perfect setting for the imminent pre-tribulation rapture taught in the Epistles addressed to the Church.

THE TREASURE AND THE PEARL

The fifth and sixth parables of this same chapter have been interpreted to prove the mid-tribulation view of the rapture.

"Again, the kingdom of heaven is like unto treasure hid in a field; the which when a man hath found, he hideth, and for joy thereof goeth and selleth all that he hath, and buyeth that field. Again, the kingdom of heaven is like unto a merchant man, seeking goodly pearls: who, when he had found one pearl of great price, went and sold all that he had, and bought it" (Matt. 13:44-46).

It is said that in the parable of the treasure hid in the field, Jesus taught the regathering and reclaiming of Israel from her present world-wide dispersion in the field. Of the parable of the pearl of great price, it is said: "In this parable Jesus teaches the completion of the Church, formed through suffering, at such great cost, and the claiming of her by the One whose she is by purchase right." Because everything in Matthew 13 is said to be in exact order, these two happenings of the end time are to occur in this order.

The first objection to this reasoning is that these parables are figurative language. It is contrary to the laws of logic to use figurative language as proof. It should only be used as explanation. Why? Because figurative language must be interpreted. Thus the interpretation becomes the proof. If the interpretation is wrong, as in this case, the conclusion is wrong.

Granting that Israel is the treasure and the world is the field this parable teaches nothing more than the purchase of the field with Israel hidden therein. Not a word is said in this parable to indicate "the regathering and reclaiming of Israel from her present . . . dispersion in the field." The parable leaves Israel hidden in the field and so Israel has been and shall be during the full time of the Church.

It is after "the fulness of the Gentiles be come in" that "all Israel shall be saved: as it is written, There shall come out of Sion the Deliverer, and shall turn away ungodliness from Jacob" (Rom. 11:25–26).

With this agree the words of James: "Simeon hath declared how God at the first did visit the Gentiles, to take out of them a people for his name. And to this agree the words of the prophets; as it is written, After this I will return and will build again the tabernacle of David" (Acts 15:14–16). It shall be after God has taken the pearl of great price out of the Gentiles that Israel shall be restored.

Yes, the order is correct. Israel is hid in the world until the Church is taken out of the world and that is all these parables teach.

The fallacy of the given interpretation was due to a failure to seek a direct statement in the Word of God in its support. Because no such verse was given, the sole authority for the interpretation is that of the one by whom it has been offered.

CHAPTER 21

Miscellaneous Arguments Answered

KEPT FROM THE HOUR OF TRIAL

ONE of the great promises to the Church is that spoken to the Church at Philadelphia. "I also will keep thee from the hour of temptation, which shall come upon all the world, to try them that dwell upon the earth" (Rev. 3:10). The "hour of temptation" is interpreted as referring to the tribulation. Post-tribulationists accept this interpretation, but rob the Church of its comfort by insisting that the word *ek*, in the Greek, which is translated 'from' does not mean that, but should be translated 'out of the midst of.' Moffat's translation is quoted as reading: "I will keep you safe through the hour of trial," and Goodspeed's as: "Keep you safe in the time of testing." It is, however, admitted that not all competent scholars give the word *ek* this meaning.

The Authorized Version, the American Standard Version, the Revised Standard Version of 1946, and the Douay Version translated from the Latin Vulgate, all adhere to the preposition *from*. Each of these four translations was made by a group of scholars cooperating with each other. This excludes the influence of a personal bias on any translations made by an individual. These translations by groups of men must represent a broader scholarship than those quoted in support of the post-tribulation view. It seems then that, judging this promise by the test of scholarship, the pre-tribulation interpretation has the greater support.

But scholarship is not the final test of the meaning of a text. God says "that no prophecy of the scripture is of any private interpretation." This means that no verse shall be interpreted apart from that which is elsewhere written. That is the test to which the promise to the Church at Philadelphia must be put. Are there any other Scripture passages that teach that the Church shall be kept from passing through that time? Are there any passages that affirm that the Church shall be in the tribulation but kept from harm during it?

Paul wrote: "For God hath not appointed us unto wrath, but to obtain salvation by our Lord Jesus Christ . . . that . . . we should live together with him" (1 Thess. 5:9–10). The wrath here includes the wrath of the day of the Lord and therefore the wrath of the tribulation. Salvation here is "that . . . we should live together with him." The context (4:17) clearly shows that living together with Him will be when the Church is caught up to meet Him in the air. This is deliverance from, not out of, or through.

Paul, in Romans 9:22–23, clearly teaches, as has previously been said, that God endures with much long-suffering the vessels of wrath fitted to destruction, so that He might make known the riches of His glory on the vessels of mercy (the Church) which He has prepared unto glory. The riches of God's glory will not be made known until the Church has been glorified at the rapture. When that will be accomplished, He will pour His wrath upon the vessels of wrath. And that is during the tribulation. If this teaches anything it is that the Church will be kept from, yes completely exempt from, the hour of trial.

The two foregoing passages are sufficient to show that *ek* in Revelation 3:10 means *from*.

An effort has been made to support, by a Scripture passage, the interpretation of *ek* as meaning 'keep safe through.' It is said that Revelation 12:6, 14 "reveal the possibility and certainty of a people in relationship with God being thus preserved from the Great Tribulation." The people here referred to is Israel. This is not denied. The point emphasized is that "a holy people in relationship to God can be exempted from the last tribulation, without being taken up to heaven by a rapture." Notice carefully that all that is said in the two above-mentioned quotations is that God *can* preserve a holy people through the tribulation. But *that is not the issue.* No one will deny God's ability to do so. The issue is, does He say that He will do so with the Church? *He does not.* As shown in Chapter 13 it is repeatedly said that God will provide safekeeping for Israel through the tribulation but not a single time is it said that He will so keep the Church. It has also been shown that God has a reason and a purpose for so keeping Israel, but again no reason or purpose for so keeping the Church can be found.

God has said that He will show the riches of His

glory upon the Church *before* He pours His wrath, during the tribulation, upon the vessels of wrath. What point is it, then, to confuse the issue by arguing that God can do something contrary to that which His word teaches He will do? Here is seen one more weakness of the post-tribulation arguments, a distortion of the plain and simple meaning of God's Word.

CHURCH HAS ALWAYS GONE THROUGH TRIBULATION

One of the arguments used in support of the claim that the Church will pass through the tribulation is that during its history it has repeatedly passed through tribulation. One writer has said: "Surely the Church has been permitted to pass through many other periods of suffering and anguish so acute that if those who went through them should have to go through the tribulation, they should not feel they had missed anything during their first period of trial." This statement is nothing more than loose thinking, pure human speculation. Absolutely no proof can be found in it. Just because a given condition has existed in the past is no reason that it will so continue in the future. A conclusion must be based on two premises to be proof. The foregoing statement contains only one. No passage from the Word of God is quoted to support the supposed conclusion. Furthermore, *the tribulation* is something entirely different from tribulation which the Church suffers in the world.

Here are two more statements expressing the

speculative thinking of post-tribulationists about the awfulness of the tribulation. "If Jacob is not having trouble now, as we think of the millions of Jews in Europe that are being slowly or suddenly exterminated, who knows what trouble is?" "Certainly we have no assurance it will be worse than much of the suffering already experienced." Let it be said again, no word of God is offered to support these statements. Both are pure human speculations. In fact the last one is a direct denial of the words of Jesus. Is there no assurance that the tribulation will be worse than suffering already experienced? Jesus said: "For then shall be great tribulation, such as was not since the beginning of the world to this time, no, nor ever shall be. And except those days should be shortened, there should no flesh be saved" (Matt. 24:21–22). What more assurance is needed? In addition, twice in the Old Testament, Joel 2:2 and Jeremiah 30:5–7, God made similar statements. When will men stop contradicting the words of Jesus by saying things cannot be worse than in Europe during World War II or during the ten Roman persecutions of the early Church? Even the atomic bomb and the hydrogen bomb contradict these statements by post-tribulationists.

It is further argued that because Jesus said, "In the world ye shall have tribulation" (John 16:33), that the Church will go through the tribulation. Not a word is said here to indicate that the Church will be in the world at the time of unprecedented tribulation.

The words, "that we must through much tribulation enter into the kingdom of God" (Acts 14:22),
are also quoted as proof that the Church will pass
through the tribulation. To hold this and to use any
verses which declare that tribulation shall be experienced by the Church is to ignore entirely the
difference between the tribulation referred to in
these verses and the great tribulation.

This suffering of the Church due to present tribulation is not inconsistent with God's love for her.
Whom the Lord loveth He chasteneth. This chas-
tening is that it might bear the peaceable fruit of
righteousness (Heb. 12:6, 11). And Peter wrote that
manifold temptations were to try the faith, as gold is
tried by fire, so that it might be unto praise and
honor and glory at the appearing of Jesus Christ
(1 Pet. 1:6–7)

The tribulation is vastly different. At least the last
part of it will be the day of the Lamb's wrath. That
which is done by the Lamb in wrath is judgment and
punishment and is completely void of love.

The mid-tribulationist recognizes this and therefore tries to prove that the Church will be raptured
in the middle of the seven-year period before the
day of the Lamb's wrath comes.

The post-tribulationist argues that because God
is going to protect and bring Israel through the tribulation, God can also protect and bring the Church
through the same period. Here again, as so often in
post-tribulation writings, is a conclusion based on
only one premise. Because God can is absolutely no

proof that there shall be occasion for Him to do so. He has repeatedly said in both Old and New Testaments that He will protect Israel. He has never said that He will protect the Church. Why? Because, as has been shown, the Church shall not pass through that day of wrath.

THE SAVED OUT OF THE TRIBULATION

The "great multitude, which no man could number, of all nations, and kindreds, and people, and tongues" that John saw standing before the Lamb, clothed in white robes, and palms in their hands (Rev. 7:9), are said by post-tribulationists to be the Church. In verse 14 it is said of them that they came out of great tribulation. This is offered as proof that the Church must pass through the tribulation.

In the first place, it is impossible for this great multitude to be the Church. Only the last living generation of the Church could pass through *great* tribulation. All other generations will have died before the great tribulation begins. These cannot possibly pass through that period. At the most, even if the post-tribulation view were correct, this multitude can only include that last generation. This leaves all other generations of the Church to be accounted for otherwise. Will there be two separate groups of the Church in heaven? The Bible does not so teach. Paul clearly taught that the dead in Christ and the living believers shall be caught up in one group.

The simple meaning of Revelation 7:9–17 is that out of the great tribulation period shall come a great multitude of saved persons who are to serve God in His temple day and night. The fact that the Church shall be the bride of Christ disqualifies her for this service. Jesus said to His disciples: "Henceforth I call you not servants . . . but I have called you friends." The heavenly position of the Church shall not be that of servants.

These servants in the temple of God will hold the same position as the Levites, the servants in the temple at Jerusalem. The Church shall share the glory of Jesus Christ. Jesus said: "The glory which thou gavest me I have given them" (John 17:22). Such glory is not given to an order of servants. The Church shall reign with Him (2 Tim. 2:12). The Church shall judge the world and angels (1 Cor. 6:1-2). These are not functions of the servants in the temple.

The question has been asked, How can any be saved during the tribulation if the Holy Spirit is taken from the earth? This is only one of a considerable number of similar questions asked by post-tribulationists. The asking of this question leaves the implication that the Holy Spirit will not be taken out of the way, as is claimed by those who hold the pre-tribulation view. But it must be remembered that men were saved throughout the Old Testament times before the Holy Spirit was sent by Christ to indwell believers. That He, as indwelling believers, shall be taken out of the way as a restraint upon lawlessness does not mean that men cannot be saved as they were before He thus came.

It has also been said that there will be no witness for Christ during the tribulation if the Church is not left on earth. This statement shows a serious lack of knowledge of God's Word. In the 144,000 Israelites, servants of God, is seen a faithful witness during that time.

AT THE LAST TRUMP

In support of the mid-tribulation view the expression "At the last trump" of 1 Corinthians 15:52 has been said to be the trumpet sounded by the seventh angel as recorded in Revelation 11:15–19. This trumpet has been made the determining factor in fixing the time of the rapture. It has been said that it will be sounded in the middle of the tribulation.

It is difficult to understand how the sounding of this trumpet can be said to be in the middle of the tribulation. When this trumpet was sounded, John heard "great voices in heaven, saying, The kingdoms of this world are become the kingdoms of our Lord, and of his Christ; and he shall reign for ever and ever." Will this be true in the middle of the tribulation, at the time that the man of sin sets himself in the temple and is worshipped as God? The kingdoms of the world will not become the kingdoms of Christ until after the Battle of Armageddon at the end of the tribulation.

The "last trump" of 1 Corinthians 15:52 must be the same as the trump of 1 Thessalonians 4:16 because at both the dead in Christ are said to be raised. But the trump in Thessalonians, as explained in Chapter 12, is said to be "the trump of God" and the Lord *Himself* shall descend with that trump. That trump will not be sounded by an angel. It is evident, then, that the trumpet of the seventh angel cannot be the "last trump" of 1 Corinthians 15:52 and also that it will not be sounded in the middle of the tribulation.

IS THE ROMAN EMPIRE HE THAT RESTRAINETH?

The interpretation of 2 Thessalonians 2:6–7 that the One who restrains until he be taken out of the way is the Holy Spirit has been said to be merely an ingenious but precarious conjecture. To get away from the Holy Spirit as the restrainer, post-tribulationists are forced to offer an argument that not only is a conjecture but one for which *not a single word of Scripture can be offered*. It has even been admitted "that any solution of 2 Thess. 2:6–7 must be conjectural; the best of the conjectures is the one that comes down from Tertullian and Chrysostom."

The following is the *admitted conjecture* of the post-tribulationists. Here are the words of one writer: "Some have believed that the hindering influence is that of law and order as embodied in the Roman Empire. It is argued with considerable cogency, that Paul was purposely enigmatic and reminded the Thessalonians what they knew very well, from previous instructions he had given them, just what the restraining influence was in their day, namely the Roman Empire. Paul naturally refrained from being specific on paper because he did not wish to endanger the Christian movement by laying it open to charges of sedition through teaching that the system of Roman law and order would some day break down." Talk about a *precarious* conjecture! What could be more precarious than to conjecture the motive of a man who wrote generations before one's time? And not the slightest attempt is made to support this by the Scriptures. This appears to be the best explanation of 2 Thessalonians 2:6–7 the post-tribulationists have to offer.

It is well to examine this view. What kind of lawlessness did the Roman system at best restrain? Nothing more than civil lawlessness—the breaking of human laws. That is all. What kind of lawlessness is restrained by Him of whom Paul wrote? It is spiritual; it is lawlessness against God. After the Restrainer is taken out of the way, the lawless one shall set himself up against God and be worshipped as God. Did the Roman Empire restrain spiritual lawlessness? It did not. Christians were martyred because they refused to call the emperor Lord. The lawless one will demand just that recognition when the Restrainer is taken out of the way.

It must not be overlooked that the Roman Empire was one of the kingdoms the devil offered Jesus if He would fall down and worship Him. Rome, belonging to the domain of Satan, could hardly be said to restrain the coming one who will be empowered by Satan.

Again, Paul clearly spoke of the restraint as being, not only by an impersonal influence but, also by a person. Paul said: "Until he be taken out of the way." That cannot apply to any system of law nor to any nation. To get around this, it has been suggested that this refers to the Roman emperors. But "he" is in the singular and cannot refer to more than one person, and that person was restraining when Paul wrote and is still restraining today, nineteen hundred years later.

The year 476 has been said to mark, perhaps better than any other, the fall of the Roman empire in the West. But post-tribulationists are not dismayed by this. The restraining influence is said to be carried on by the Holy Roman Empire even down to 1806 at which time it is acknowledged that it, too, died. But how about the century and a half that has passed since then? A post-tribulationist still has an answer. "Roman law and Roman justice are still a barrier, and the Emperors live on in the Papacy."

And so the Papacy becomes the restrainer? How interesting! The Papacy is the church. But is it the true Church or the apostate? Remember, the restrainer shall be taken out of the way before the lawless one is revealed. If the Papacy is the true Church then the Church will be taken away before the lawless one is revealed in perfect harmony with the pre-tribulation view. Therefore, the post-tribulation view is shown to be false. But if the Papacy belongs to the apostate church then it is not taken away before the lawless one is revealed, because it is seen judged at the end of the tribulation just before Christ comes in glory, and that will be *after* the lawless one shall be revealed. But the Bible teaches that the restrainer shall be taken away *before* that time. Then the apostate Church cannot be the restrainer.

So by a series of conjectures, born of human speculation, at least one well recognized post-tributionist has brought himself face to face with a dilemma, both horns of which are completely damaging to his position.

The foregoing is supposed to be Bible interpretation. It seems to be the best that the post-tributionists have to offer in refutation of the pre-tribution explanation that He who restrains is the Holy Spirit and that which restrains is the Church. It is completely damaging to their position.

THE TWO WITNESSES

Post-tributionists, feeling a need for a fixed event at which to locate the rapture, place it at Matthew 24:30–31. So, also, the mid-tribulation view needs an event at which the Church will be caught up. This has been supposed to be found in the ascension of the two witnesses in Revelation 11:12: "And they heard a great voice from heaven saying unto them, Come up hither. And they ascended up to heaven in a cloud; and their enemies beheld them."

Because these two witnesses shall have been dead and raised from death is the only reason given why they represent the Church. Because they are two they are supposed to represent the dead in Christ that shall be raised and the living saints that shall be caught up with them at the Lord's coming.

The reasons why these cannot represent the Church are so apparent that no one should be misled by this claim. First of all, there shall be two of them. The Church is one body, not two. The Church will not be raptured as two bodies. Then, both witnesses were killed and raised from the dead. Neither can represent the living saints at the Lord's coming. Once more, their dead bodies shall lie in the street of Jerusalem for three days. How does that apply to the Church? But, most of all, their ministry is the very opposite to that of the Church preaching the Gospel of grace. They shall "have power to shut heaven, that it rain not . . . and have power over waters to turn them to blood, and to smite the earth with all plagues, as often as they will" (v. 6). And if any one would hurt them fire shall come out of their mouths to destroy their enemies. And these have been said to represent the Church! Never!

In reading Revelation one cannot help but feel that the three and a half years of ministry of these witnesses shall be during the latter part of the tribulation and their ascension to heaven near the end of it. Surely there is nothing to show that their ministry will be during the first half of that time as it must be if they represent a mid-tribulation rapture.

No event recorded in Revelation can better represent the rapture of the Church than that found in Chapter 4:1. It follows immediately the messages to the seven Churches in which is seen a preview of the Church age, and is followed by all the events of the tribulation, "things which must be hereafter."

John heard a voice talking to him which said: "Come up hither." Why is it fitting that this should be a type of the rapture of the Church? John was one of the eleven disciples to whom Jesus made the promise that He would come again and receive them unto Himself. More than that, he was one of the three of the inner circle of the disciples. Not only that, he is the only one of whom it was said that he leaned on Jesus' bosom. He is described as the disciple that Jesus loved. So also the Church is the special object of the love of Christ. The name *John* is also significant. It means "Jehovah hath been gracious." That too is descriptive of the Church. In that John alone is called up to heaven is seen the unity of the Church as one body. Who could better typify the Church than John?

This is not offered as proof of the pre-tribulation rapture, because types are not proofs, but if one is seeking an event from the record in Revelation that has within itself the characteristics of the rapture of the Church none other as good can be found.

CHAPTER 22

When Shall the Dead in Christ Be Raised?

IN ORDER to prove a post-tribulation rapture it becomes necessary to prove a post-tribulation resurrection of the Church, because the resurrection and the rapture shall take place in the same "twinkling of an eye." A post-tribulation resurrection requires a post-tribulation parousia. It has already been shown, in Chapter 8, that the parousia will be before the sudden destruction of the day of the Lord and in Chapter 18 that it will not be at the coming of the Son of man in the clouds of heaven. Because the parousia shall be before the tribulation, the resurrection and the rapture must also come before that time. This alone is sufficient to prove a pre-tribulation resurrection. Because of the extended arguments offered in support of the post-tribulation view it is well to examine some of the devious statements that have been made in order to locate the resurrection after the tribulation.

It has been said that Jesus taught that the resurrection will be when the Son of man comes in the clouds of heaven after the tribulation. As authority for this the words of Jesus, "I will raise him up at the last day" (John 6:39–40, 44, 54) are quoted.

It is claimed that "the last day" is the last of the

"pre-Messianic Age." In support of this it is said: "the Jews divided time into two ages, the Messianic Age, and that which preceded it." But in John 6 Jesus taught Church truth, not Jewish, and therefore the Jewish division of time cannot be used as conclusive evidence.

If one bears in mind that Jesus was teaching Church truth when He made the statement, "I will raise him up at the last day," it becomes evident that the last day is that of the interim period between the sixty-ninth and seventieth weeks of Israel during which God is calling out a people for His name's sake. Against this it has been contended that the time the Church is on earth is not an age. What of it? Every period of time longer than one day has a last day. Jesus did not say at the last day of the age. Thus it is seen that a highly debatable point at best is used as basic to prove that Jesus taught a post-tribulation resurrection of the Church.

But that is not the most serious error in this contention. The four following quotations found within four pages show a most extraordinary method of argumentation:

"And having regard to His [i.e., Jesus'] fundamental ideas on Eschatology there can be no doubt that 'the last day' is the closing day of the Age that precedes the Messianic kingdom of glory." "It is the last day of this present evil Age, the first of the Age to come." "The resurrection of the just is the first result of the Messianic reign." "For just as the last note of one octave is the first note of the next, so the last day of this present Age is the first of the Messianic Age to follow."

Ask any orthodox Jew if the last day of the week, his Sabbath, is the same as the first day of the week, the Christian's Lord's day. That which is true of the octave is not true of any period of time.

This is nothing less than twisting the words of Jesus to make them fit one's own preconceived idea of what He should have said. All this is done to make Jesus teach that the resurrection of the Church shall be when the Son of man comes in the clouds of heaven after the tribulation. *At no time did Jesus teach that the resurrection of the Church shall come after the tribulation.* He taught that it will be "at the last day" and that shall come before the Messianic kingdom begins. *That is not the first day.* Because He was teaching Church truth when He made this statement, it is more logical to consider it the last day of the Christian era than that of the Jewish pre-Messianic era. In any event, it cannot be within the Messianic age when the Son of man comes in the clouds of heaven.

It has been said that Paul, also, taught that the resurrection of the Church will be when the Son of man comes in the clouds of heaven. In 1 Thessalonians 4:15–17 Paul taught that the resurrection of the dead in Christ will be the first event at the parousia of the Lord. Then in 5:1–3 he related the parousia to the coming of the day of the Lord. It follows then that the resurrection of the dead in Christ shall be at the *coming* of the day of the Lord.

At least one ardent post-tribulationist admits, in fact strongly contends, that the resurrection will be related to the day of the Lord. He has said: "We have already seen that, alike in the teaching of the Prophets, and the Lord Jesus Christ, of Paul and the apocalypse, the resurrection of the saints is located with the utmost definiteness at the Day of the Lord." And again: "The time of the Rapture must stand or fall with the time of the saints' resurrection; and this is located at the Day of the Lord." What is more, it is said that "The fundamental point in the inquiry concerns the relation of the rapture of the risen and transfigured saints, to the Day of the Lord."

The last of these three statements is true. The relation of the resurrection and the rapture to the day of the Lord becomes a fundamental point at issue. The present question then is, What did Paul teach about the time of the parousia and the resurrection of believers? This has been explained elsewhere, but inasmuch as it is fundamental to the entire issue, repetition thereof might be helpful.

Paul wrote: "For . . . the day of the Lord so cometh as a thief in the night. For when they shall say, Peace and safety; then sudden destruction cometh upon them, as travail upon a woman with child; and they shall not escape" (1 Thess. 5:2–3). This is the event to which Paul relates the resurrection. This must be the very beginning of the day of the Lord.

The event to which the post-tribulationists relate the resurrection is that described by Jesus. "Im-

mediately after the tribulation of those days . . .
shall appear the sign of the Son of man in heaven:
and then shall all the tribes of the earth mourn, and
they shall see the Son of man coming in the clouds of
heaven with power and great glory."

Paul pictured a scene of darkness and destruction
coming secretly and at a time of apparent peace and
safety. Jesus pictured a scene of light and manifest
glory and power coming immediately after the
greatest tribulation of human history.

That which Paul described will be the beginning
of that part of the day of the Lord foretold by the
Old Testament prophets when the destruction of the
Lord shall come upon the earth, when He shall
punish the wicked for their sins and cleanse the land
of sinners. It includes the day of the wrath of the
Lord and, as has previously been explained, coincides with the tribulation period.

That which Jesus described follows the tribulation, and will be the beginning of the establishment
of peace on earth.

It is difficult to see how these two can be said to
describe the same event except for the need of a post-
tribulation parousia and a post-tribulation day of
the Lord in order to provide an argument for a post-
tribulation rapture. Here, again, is an illustration of
the extent to which the Scriptures have been dis-
torted in an effort to prove the post-tribulation view.

The Apocalypse is also said to contain evidence of
a post-tribulation resurrection of the Church saints.
Revelation 11:15–18, in which is told that which

shall come to pass at the sounding of the trumpet by the seventh angel, is offered as evidence. The following quotations show the reasoning of a post-tribulationist: "Here we have once again the resurrection of the saints. Paul tells us that the dead in Christ shall be raised at the Last Trumpet." "We have already seen that this trumpet sounds on the Day of the Lord when Israel is converted and the kingdom introduced. And here in Rev. XI:15, we have these very events under the seventh or last trumpet, which also blows at the Day of the Lord. The conclusion is inevitable, therefore, that the Last Trumpet of Paul, and the Last Trumpet of John, are one and the same. We are right, therefore, in inferring the resurrection from Rev. XI:15–18."

The above is not as conclusive as that writer wishes one to believe. The trumpet at which the dead in Christ shall arise according to Paul is the trump of God and Paul said clearly, so that no one should misunderstand, that the Lord Himself and no other descends from heaven with that trump. To say that the trumpet sounded by an angel is the same as one ascribed to the Lord Himself is not a convincing argument.

Again, it is said that the seventh trumpet is sounded at the day of the Lord by which is meant the time when the Son of man shall come in the clouds of heaven. Paul related the descent of the Lord from heaven with the trump of God to the *beginning* of the day of the Lord, when they shall say peace and safety and sudden destruction shall come. This cannot, as has repeatedly been said, co-incide with the coming in the clouds with power and great glory.

Nothing requires the Church to be in view in this passage. "Thy servants the prophets" is a term describing the Old Testament prophets. Because the Church saints will be in heaven as the bride of the Lamb at that time, the saints of this passage must be either Israel or those saved during the tribulation.

Because of the divergent interpretation to which this passage has been subject, it is clear that it cannot be used to establish so important a doctrine as the time of the resurrection. In fact, the true interpretation of this passage requires a previous knowledge of the time of the resurrection and the rapture.

Revelation 20:4–6 is also quoted as evidence of a post-tribulation rapture. Verses 4 and 5 are here quoted: "And I saw thrones, and they sat upon them, and judgment was given unto them: and I saw the souls of them that had been beheaded for the testimony of Jesus, and for the word of God, and such as worshipped not the beast, neither his image, and received not the mark upon their forehead and upon their hand; and they lived, and reigned with Christ a thousand years. The rest of the dead lived not until the thousand years should be finished. This is the first resurrection" (A.S.V.).

This passage has been said to be the *clearest possible* refutation of the pre-tribulation view. The reason given is that "according to this vision of the Apocalypse, the first resurrection takes place in the

immediate association with the destruction of Antichrist, and the establishment of the Messianic Kingdom. . . . Nothing can be found of an earlier one,
either here or in any other part of the Word of God."

The last part of the above statement is not true.
Paul taught that God will show the riches of His
glory upon the vessels of mercy before the long-
suffering of God comes to an end and His wrath will
fall on the vessels of wrath (Rom. 9:22–23). The
glorification of the Church requires a previous resurrection. The wrath of the Lamb falls at the opening
of the sixth seal (Rev. 6:17) and that will be before
the resurrection of Revelation 20:5. Yes, Paul did
know of a resurrection of the Church before this
"first resurrection."

Again, Paul taught the resurrection of the dead in
Christ at the parousia and Jesus placed the parousia
before any destruction shall come upon the world.
Paul also taught that the parousia shall be before
the *coming* of the day of the Lord, not seven years
later when the Son of man comes in the clouds of
heaven to establish the Messianic kingdom. Here,
then, is seen a threefold evidence of a resurrection
of the Church about seven years before the "first
resurrection" of Revelation 20:5.

The explanation by pre-tribulationists that there
are at least two parts to the first resurrection is ridiculed. But why not. The harvest in the Old Testament consisted of the first-fruits, the harvest, and the
gleanings—three separate parts. Because the resurrection of Christ is said to be the "firstfruits" (1 Cor.

15:20) it is safe to say that the Old Testament harvest is a type of the resurrection of God's people. The harvest proper and the gleanings represent two *separate* events, but both are said to be the harvest. Inasmuch as the Bible clearly teaches the resurrection of God's people at two separated times it is most reasonable to compare these with the harvest proper and the gleanings. Because the resurrection of Christ, the "firstfruits," has been separated from the coming harvest by more than nineteen hundred years, the separation of the gleanings from the harvest by about seven years should not seem unreasonable. The type here explains how there can be two separated events to the "first resurrection." The clear teaching of the Word is that there will be two events.

In further explanation of this passage in support of the post-tribulation view, it is said that three distinct classes are seen in this passage. The first class John saw was those that sat upon thrones. These are said to be "the whole body of saints who live to see the Parousia at this time," which is after the tribulation. Here the forced and unbiblical interpretation of the arrival aspect of the parousia creates an impossible condition. Because the parousia was by Jesus located before any destruction came upon the unsuspecting peoples of the earth, none of the Church saints will live through the tribulation to see it after that time. This interpretation also gives to those of the Church who live to the coming of the Lord a special advantage over those who have gone to sleep in Christ.

The second class are those of whom John wrote: "I saw the souls of them that had been beheaded for the testimony of Jesus, and for the word of God." These are said to be the dead in Christ who shall be raised when the Lord descends from heaven according to 1 Thessalonians 4:16. It is "strongly insisted upon that 'beheaded for the testimony of Jesus and for the word of God' is a description, and a glorious description, of the martyrdom of a Christian." While this may, or may not, be true, it is not the slightest proof that this passage refers to Church martyrs. If that were so, where are all the millions of members of the Church that for centuries have fallen asleep by natural death? Not a trace of them is found in this passage. This, surely, is straining a point in an effort to prove a desired conclusion.

The simple explanation of this class is that they are "the souls of them that were slain for the word of God, and the testimony which they held" (Rev. 6:9). The use of the unusual expression "the souls of them" to identify these persons in both verses supports the simple explanation of the passage.

More might be said but this is sufficient to show that these passages quoted in support of the post-tribulation view are subject to other interpretations and must themselves be tested by that which is taught elsewhere.

And these debatable interpretations are offered as proof of the admitted basic point of the post-tribulation view!

All passages that speak of the resurrection must be

tested by the fact that the resurrection of the Church shall be at the parousia and that shall be before the destruction of the tribulation falls upon an unsuspecting world (Matt. 24:35–37). A second test is that the dead in Christ shall be raised before the *coming* of the day of the Lord as described by Paul (1 Thess. 5:2–3). A third test is that the resurrection of the Church and rapture must come before the wrath of God falls upon the vessels of wrath because the Church shall be glorified before that occurs (Rom. 9:22–23). Any passage that does not meet these tests must not be interpreted as describing the resurrection of Church saints.

Any system of eschatology (the doctrine of last things) that must be built on as questionable interpretations as the above and many others previously considered does not have much to commend itself.